HILL RUNNING

Survive & Thrive

JEFF GRANT

COACH

HILLSEEKER®

Hill Running: Survive & Thrive

Copyright @2018 by Jeffrey Scott Grant

Cover designed by Oswald V. Cameron, www.oswaldcameron.com

Professional Strength Training and Running Technique photos taken by Michael Bissig of Adventure & Lifestyle Photography in Switzerland, mikebite.com. All other photos by the Author and/or owned by the Author.

Mountains Sketch Art by Aditya, @bananamonkeii on Instagram. Editing graciously provided by Kiston Finney.

ISBN: 978-3-9524667-6-6

Published in Switzerland by Hillseeker Publishing, a division of Hillseeker Fitness GmbH. Hillseeker.com

10 9 8 7 6 5 4 3 2 1
First Edition

Disclaimer

You must get your physician's approval before beginning the physically demanding elements covered in this book, especially if you have any medical condition or injury that contraindicates physical activity. This program is designed for healthy individuals 18 years and older. These recommendations are not medical guidelines but are for educational purposes only.

The information in this book is meant to supplement, not replace, proper exercise training. All forms of exercise pose some inherent risks. The author advises readers to take full responsibility for their safety and know their limits.

Before practicing the exercises in this book, be sure that your equipment is well maintained, and do not take risks beyond your level of experience, aptitude, training and fitness. The exercises and programs in this book are not intended as a substitute for any exercise routine or treatment that may have been prescribed by your physician.

See your physician before starting any exercise program. If you are taking any medications, you must talk to your physician before starting any exercise program. If you experience any lightheadedness, dizziness, or shortness of breath while exercising, stop the movement and consult a physician.

Don't perform any exercise unless you have been shown the proper technique by a certified personal trainer or certified strength and conditioning specialist. Always do a warm-up prior to strength training and interval training.

You must have a complete physical examination if you are sedentary, if you have high cholesterol, high blood pressure, or diabetes, if you are overweight, or if you are over 30 years old.

If your physician recommends against any of these workouts, please follow those orders.

Table of Contents

Introduction

"It is not the mountain we conquer but ourselves." — Sir Edmund Hillary

Running Hills in the Berner Oberland, Switzerland

Hills: a powerful teacher

Sometimes you get it wrong, very wrong. And sometimes you get it right, very right. I experienced both in consecutive years at a classic ultra marathon in Switzerland, the 78KM Swiss Alpine Marathon. These experiences offered such valuable lessons in hill training and the hill running mindset that their contrasting stories make for a powerful opener for this training guide.

Year 1 -- Getting it Wrong

The first marathon seems easy, too easy. In the heart of the Swiss Alps, the route from Davos to Filisur follows a gentle gradient down for 30KM, before climbing up to small village of Bergün to finish the first 42KM of the day.

I feel strong. I should have seeded myself closer to the front of the field. Too many runners are slowly plodding in my way. It is crowded and frustrating. I pass them by running up on the sides of the road and trail — taking ankle-turning risk after ankle-turning risk for a chance at an open path. How great it feels to be this strong! I reel in pack after pack, reaching clusters of runners and then zigzagging through them or springing off trail to bound off rocks and re-enter the trail in front of them. Eventually the crowds thin and I have open trail. I run faster. Down, down, down. This is awesome. Today is my day to fly!

I blaze through 30KM at record pace and reach the 42KM banner with a time that would make me proud on a road marathon, much less the half-way point in a trail marathon that includes a massive climb and descent in its second half.

Climbing out of Bergün, my right quad begins to feel tight and my pace slows abruptly from run, to speed hike, to walk. I attempt to shake it off, taking a moment to stretch and hydrate. I probably should have been drinking and eating more the past few hours, but I was enjoying the running too much to be bothered. I struggle to regain my run. My legs are heavy and getting heavier by the minute. A few runners pass me. This is ok. I just need another minute to hydrate and have a snack, and I'll be fine.

The walking continues, and the real climb begins … 1300M of elevation gain in 10KM of distance up to Keschhütte. I try to run again, but my legs aren't working. Worse, my walking pace is slowing dramatically. Runners and walkers are passing me- -tens…dozens…hundreds — all of whom I passed during my overly-excited opening marathon today. They are passing me as if I'm sitting down in the middle of the trail.

Am I? Am I standing still? It sure feels like it.

I will myself to continue my slow walk up the mountain, while listening to a negative voice in my head, my Inner Critic, try to persuade me to abandon the race[1]. I stop many times to stretch and to listen to this negative dialogue in my mind, a dialogue that tells me today isn't my day and that it is time to cut

The Melt Down: Walking at the Swiss Alpine Marathon

my losses and try again next year without suffering through another 5+ hours of pain just to finish the race with a lousy time.

Somehow, I manage to ignore my Inner Critic long enough to reach the top of this major climb, where I arrive at a support station and find myself surrounded by other runners, some appearing fresh and energized, and others looking as wrecked as I feel. I drink some warm tea and persuade myself to continue.

---

[1] Inner Critic and Inner Coach are two key concepts I teach in *Flow State Runner*.

The high alpine single-track trail section between high passes is my favorite of the race, and I want to attempt to run it, in hopes that it will lift my spirits. But not today. I'm stuck in a queue of runners who are carefully stepping through shallow streams and rocky sections, resulting in a slowly-moving conga line. I patiently walk this section, feeling my optimism fade and another energetic crash incoming. My walking again slows to a crawl, and once again I contemplate abandoning the race.

At the top of the final climb, I eat a quick snack and then set off on a painful descent, nearly 20KM long, into the finishing town of Davos. It hurts to run. It hurts to walk. Everything is happening in slow motion. Eventually, I finish—barely within the cut-off—and with a now heavy rucksack full of lessons learned.

Running strong a year later: Swiss Alpine Marathon

Year 2 -- Getting it Right

With a year of smart hill training under my belt and specific tactics in mind for each section of the course, I seed myself closer to the front of the field at the race start. I smile as I run through Davos, knowing that today I will rely more on wisdom than hubris as I attempt this stunning mountain course for the second time.

I take it easy on the initial marathon, covering it about 10 minutes longer than last year, and without the zigzagging past slower runners that overly taxed and stressed me last year. My body and mind are much more relaxed. I feel strong today.

I run and speed-hike the climb to Keschhütte energetically, confounded at how hard it felt last year. I quickly run past my numerous meltdown spots from the previous attempt. More important than my overall time and standing is the feeling I receive from running the single-track section at the top, with an open trail, as fast as I wish, hopping from rock to rock, over streams and with such freedom that I

feel I can take flight over the mountains in any of the many magical moments.

I reach the top of the final climb feeling alive and energized, and then soar down the long mountain descent to reach the finish line in Davos: 2.5 hours **faster** than last year.

In my first attempt I got things very wrong, but I learned from the experience, changed my training approach, race plan, and mindset. And consequently, on the second attempt I got things very right. I aim to teach YOU how to accomplish the same in your running, without having to get it very wrong first!

Thriving in the hills:
Swiss Alpine Marathon

Speaking of You

Do you thrive when running in hilly terrain?

Are you motivated to *survive* the hilly sections of a race, or an event that is entirely in the mountains?

Do you incorporate hill training into your conditioning program regularly?

Does the sight of a hill on the path ahead sometimes zap your energy before you even reach the incline?

Do you know how to train for hills even when you don't have them?

Do you use hills as an opportunity to practice and improve your running technique?

Are you ready to take on more challenges in your life, with the belief that challenges bring growth, even at a micro level?

I hope that the answer to at least one of those questions is yes, but even if not (yet), hang with me, as we're going on a journey up and down some virtual hills as I teach you how to get more out of the inclines in your path.

I love hills, from the smallest of rises in elevation to enormous mountains. They bring me energy and adventure. For decades as a runner, I've incorporated physical hills into my training, and virtual hills in my adventurous path in life. I also use hills extensively in my coaching practice. This is all no surprise given that I live in Switzerland, I am the founder of a company named Hillseeker®, and I live my life with a Hillseeking mentality! But we'll get to last part in a bit. Let's first talk about the benefits of training on hills.

Why Hills?

Strength & Conditioning

Running *up* hills builds lower body strength and is a powerful conditioning accelerator. Downhill running is also an effective conditioning tool, especially when used for overspeed training: that is, to prepare your body for maintaining a new pace higher than your previous pace plateau. Whether you are running simply to improve your general fitness or with a specific endurance racing goal in mind, incorporating hill training offers a superhighway toward a fitter, faster and more resilient body.

Weighted Hill repeats near Zurich on my favorite home hill

Hill sprints in Richterswil

Mental Strength

Hills offer a built-in opportunity to test and develop mental strength and a mindset for overcoming adversity. This is notably true when introducing hill challenges where you really don't want to find them! If the thought of a steep hill suddenly appearing late in any route you are on makes you anything but happy and motivated, then it is exactly what you need to increase your mental toughness and resiliency. The more you train your mind to embrace and overcome challenges, even in micro doses, the more likely you will be to return to this place of control and confidence when ever-increasing levels of challenge and adversity appear by surprise in your future path.

Technique

I use hills in running technique workshops to highlight that form often breaks down when runners are under pressure, and that the natural tendency for many is to lean *into* a hill by bending forward at the hips, which destroys optimal form. When runners get it right on the hills, their likelihood of getting it right in other terrain is greatly increased. You can view hills as your very own Olympic Training Center, with countless tools at the ready to help you refine your posture and movement patterns under varying degrees of complexity and challenge.

Flow Enabler

Hills serve a highly effective catalyst for the Struggle phase of flow. As described in my book *Flow State Runner* and uncovered through decades of research by Dr. Mihaly Csikszentmihalyi and colleagues, flow occurs in a cycle of four stages, starting with Struggle. Hill running is a short-cut to Struggle, in that for most, it brings about sufficient challenge to release the key flow stress hormones adrenaline and cortisol, as well as norepinephrine, which boosts energy and focus.

The view and feeling at the top!

Lastly, it simply feels great to reach the top! Maybe there's a view to savor, and if so, don't allow life to rush by without savoring it for a moment. Or perhaps

Celebrating the majesty of hills, mountains, and nature with Alphorns in the Engadin, Switzerland

your summit is in a forest or the top of a flight of stairs in an office building. If that's the case, close your eyes for a moment and embrace the raw feeling of accomplishment. Then, seal it in and re-use that confidence and energy for your next challenge!

Roadmap

This book teaches you key Hill Running Techniques, spanning the critical areas of mind and body. It also provides you with a large collection of hill workouts to integrate into your training and adventures as a runner.

The lessons in *Hill Running: Survive & Thrive* are powerful independently, but also work extremely well as a companion to *Flow State Runner,* which is a comprehensive resource on preparing your mind and body for optimal running experiences.

Here's how this course unfolds:

- **Chapter 1:** Efficient hill running body position, where to look, cadence, equipment considerations, and more
- **Chapter 2:** Innovative mindset and mental strength tools to accelerate your performance on the hills
- **Chapter 3:** Strength and Conditioning for Hill Running
- **Chapter 4:** Your Hill Running Library: Thirty challenging hill workouts
- **Bonus:** Sample of 10-Week Training Plan from Expanded Online Coaching version

1. Hill Running Technique

Proper technique is crucial to your ability to <u>survive</u> in the hills. Inefficient technique in uphill running will rob you of your performance potential, as if you were wearing a weight vest and dragging a tire—both of which are excellent training tools, but they should only appear when you physically attach them to your body, not virtually when you put your body in a position that makes the hill feel much steeper than it is!

And it's not just about getting it right when going *up*. Inefficient technique downhill stands to injure you and reduce your ability to recover from training and racing efforts. The last thing we want in your running is an injury that wipes out all of your hard-won fitness gains! So, let's take a journey to shore up your skills when running both uphill and downhill. Keep in mind that there are five main facets of efficient Hill Running Technique:

1. Body Position
2. Where you Look
3. Cadence
4. Muscular Tension
5. Mastering Terrain

Your mastery of each facet is your ticket to optimizing your performance running up and down hills and keeping you injury-free. I'll teach you the most important lessons in each facet. In addition, in this chapter I will also teach you how to approach weighted running and selection/use of equipment.

1. Body Position

Flow State Runner covers general running body position and physical technique in detail, including my endorsement of the Pose Method® and Dr. Nicolas Romanov's decades of research and coaching on efficient running technique. These principles for efficient running technique apply as well for uphill and downhill running. This section is a review of the key principles, with further detail added to highlight hill-specific elements.

The most important physical technique in hill running is to run with your hips open. In other words, don't bend over or fold at your waist! Many runners do this naturally on hills, as they attempt to <u>lean</u> into the hill and charge up it by pressing their head, chest, and shoulders forward toward the hill. When this lean happens by folding at the waist, the result is counter-productive, as it pushes their center of gravity backwards. This makes it harder to fall up the hill, and easier to run in place or back DOWN the hill, neither of which is the desired result.

Notice in the next photo how the runner's head and shoulders are out in front of the hips. Don't do this! Remember, lead with your head, your form is dead. Lead with your hips, you've got zip.

*But wait, are you saying to running efficiently uphill, you have to **fall** uphill?* Yes, I am! By running more upright and leading with your hips, you are utilizing one of the most effective techniques taught in the Pose Method® of Running, and it will make you

Inefficient: Too Much Forward Bend. Shoulders are out in front of hips.

Efficient: Upright torso, head and shoulders over hips

much more efficient in your uphill running endeavor. When your hips are open, the lean will actually take place from your ankles, and your hips will come along for the ride, instead of holding slowing you down as a counter-weight.

The easiest way for many runners to remember this is simply to **RUN TALL** uphill.

In addition to maintaining an upright body position, focus solely on pulling each foot straight up under your hips, as opposed to pushing off and reaching forward with your front leg extended. Hill Running is efficient when it is done with a focus on **Fall-Pull**, rather than on Push-Kick. Said more simply in my coach's voice: RUN TALL and PULL YOUR FEET.

By the way, this Fall-Pull approach is the exact same technique you use when running stairs and why running stairs serves as an excellent training tool for efficient hill running. When running upstairs,

your torso remains upright, you fall forward, and you pull your feet. Please test this out and notice how your body responds. Try it as well by using the less efficient form of leaning forward at the waist. Notice the impact. Try to extend your front leg and push off the back leg. It won't work. Running stairs forces good technique, and in doing so gives you great insights into how you can more efficiently run up hills without stairs. I encourage you to learn from this experiment and to try to transfer the feel of efficient stairs running into your hill running game.

Running stairs also gives you direct input on what your foot position should be when the foot contacts the ground. In efficient running, this landing should be on the forefoot. Notice on the stairs, that the forefoot landing happens automatically, both up and down the stairs. Try to run stairs with a heel strike. It's a no-go. But when you run stairs, do you have to TRY to land on your forefoot? No, it happens

Wrong: Knee extension on the leading leg, heel strike, inverted Y-position

Right: Forefoot landing under hip, back foot immediately pulled off the ground.

Running Stairs Reinforces Upright Body Position & Foot Pull

Classic Etch A Sketch®, useful as a visualized mind & body reset tool

automatically because 1) you are focused on pulling your feet and 2) the shape of the stairs won't allow without it being dangerous and/or uncomfortable. We want to transfer this same forefoot landing into your hill running.

One of my most useful technique reminder tricks is what I term an *"Etch-It"* drill, whereby a runner uses a drill that instantly erases inefficient movement and establishes an efficient movement pattern which they can lift-and-shift into their running. Etch-It comes from the old *Etch A Sketch*® magnetic drawing tool that you shake back-and-forth to clear.

Running stairs is an excellent *Etch-It* drill, and it does not require 1,000 stairs to reinforce good hill technique. Even a short 10-20 step staircase is enough to reinforce the feeling of an effective foot pull. Think quiet feet, with a quick pull and relaxed fall to earth.

Another effective tool for reinforcing hill technique is skipping. Skipping serves as both a conditioning tool and a natural reinforcement of an efficient pulling pattern. It is also a powerful mental *reinforcer* of the first pattern to think of whenever you reach a hill: stand tall and pull your feet.

Skipping Reinforces Upright Body Position & Trains Foot Pull

Don't forget to tap into the power of your arms. Send your elbows backwards and allow them to follow a natural movement forwards. This is an effective indirect tool for hill running —indirect in that its impact is rhythmic and psychological, more so than providing a direct propulsive force. Nonetheless, it works for many runners by encouraging them to maintain a high cadence with an upright body position. It also serves as an active expression of your strong will to conquer a hill, which makes it a valuable mindset tool as well. Just be sure that if you employ extra arm motion, that you do so under the Minimum Effective Dose guidelines in the Muscular Tension section below.

For running downhill, bend your knees to lower your center of gravity and maximize shock absorption with your soft tissue and not your joints. Think of this as assuming an athlete's posture, with knees bent and body stable and balanced. Run under yourself (which I describe in workshops as running "in the moment or today") versus in front of yourself with outstretched legs (which I describe as running "in tomorrow").

Downhill Running: Knees Bent, Lower Center of Gravity, Agile

To slow down while downhill running, simply shift your weight backwards until your body is leaning back up the hill. Continue to pull your feet until that slight backwards lean results in you running in place. Note that this is counter to the stopping approach of extending at the knee and throwing a foot forward to brake your forward progress.

You can practice effective stopping technique on flat ground by running in place, leaning forward from the hips to run forward, shifting weight to neutral to run in place again, and then shifting weight backwards to run backwards. With this mastered, your new stopping technique is simply to shift weight backwards and then to neutral, all the while pulling your feet until you reach a smooth stopping point.

2. Where to Look

When running uphill or downhill, maintain the neutral neck position of looking straight forward. This is the healthiest position for your spine and the safest position to absorb shock to the body. Use your peripheral vision to detect obstacles in your terrain. DO NOT stare at the ground when running uphill. Many runners do this in an attempt to minimize the hill or to trick their brains into forgetting it is a hill. There are better ways to win this mental battle, and I teach you these in the next chapter. If you must deviate from a neutral neck position at all when uphill running, do it by gazing slightly up and fixating on an object to help your mental game.

When running downhill, set your gaze on your line, that is your efficient path forward through various terrain obstacles (if trail running). Break any habits of looking at one obstacle at a time. Keep your gaze quiet, that is, agile and softly focused. Over-focusing and fixating on each obstacle or trail section, particularly while on a technical descent, will rob you of your agility and slow you down. Softly scan your eyes along your path. Agile eyes, agile body, agile and fast YOU.

Wrong: Runner is staring down at the ground

Wrong: Runner is looking up too high (notice the skin folds in the back of the neck)

![Right: Neutral Neck Position]

Right: Neutral Neck Position

3. Cadence

A quick cadence is imperative when hill running. Per the Pose Method's® guidelines, 180 BPM (Beats per Minute) is the minimum tempo for pulling your feet from the ground. I find it helpful to think of running uphill as if I were mountain biking uphill. On a mountain bike, to climb, you shift to an easy gear and spin at a high cadence. In running, mentally shift to an easy gear and "spin" your legs at a high cadence by pulling your feet quickly off the ground, no slower than 180 BPM.

When running downhill, continue to quickly pull your feet until you "spin out," that is reach a speed where it is no longer possible to pull your feet with control. At that point, if your longevity as a runner is important to you, slow your pace versus shifting to a bounding, joint-slamming technique.

Downhill Gaze is straight on the line of running

180 BPM

4. Muscular Tension

The concept of Minimum Effective Dose is very important to running efficiently in any terrain. Tim Ferriss drew from a pharmacology term to make an excellent point in his bestseller the *4-Hour Body*, and it's a term I'll also borrow as it perfectly describes the desired state of muscular tension we seek while running: Minimum Effective Dose or MED. Runners often fail to realize the benefits they seek because they are unconsciously keeping too much tension in the body. They may understand the mechanics of efficient running technique and strive to put their body in the right place at the right time, yet it feels awkward, forced, and far from efficient. The underlying issue is tension, excessive muscular tension to be precise.

Wrong: Too Much Tension!

Consider you're out on a lunchtime run, stressed from a busy morning of work and worried about a series of difficult meetings expected in the afternoon. During your run, you hold that stress first in the form of a clenched left fist. That tension carries itself upstream to your left shoulder and across the body to your belly and right hip. On top of this physical tension, you add to your normal work worries the self-pressure to run with perfect technique and at a specific pace, thus introducing more layers of tension. During the run, despite your best efforts, you feel tight, slow, and mechanical. Your breathing never feels smooth and easy, and now your left knee is hurting again. Argh!

The difference between an efficient run that leaves you smiling, and a frustrating run that leaves you with new layers of stress, is your awareness and management of tension. By holding on to too much tension, you are blocking your body's ability to move smoothly, lightly, and in accordance with the physical technique you're pursuing. Even worse, the tension travels to other areas of your body, increasing its negative impact with each foot strike and creating a target-rich environment for injury.

When the tension is released and reduced to its lowest level needed for the task at hand, the mind will follow, and the body will be freed to move where it needs to be and when it needs to be there. Ignore excessive tension at your own peril. Find MED and you'll find efficiency.

Envision you have a mixing board like this for your body

Wrong: Don't turn it to 11!

Right: Tension is at MED

It may help to think of tension and MED in terms of a mixing board used by sound engineers or DJs. Imagine you have a console containing many sliding buttons, known as faders or sliders, to adjust the tension in various parts of your body from Level 0 (no tension whatsoever) to Level 10 (max tension). Slider 1 is feet, Slider 2 is hamstrings, Slider 3 is upper back, and so forth. You are the engineer controlling this tension mixing board each time you run. It is your choice if you want to set all sliders to Level 3, all to Level 8, or use a mix that suits your practical and artistic needs. It is also your choice if you want to set it and leave it in place for the entire run or constantly monitor and adjust based on the evolution of your run, the change in terrain, the change in your goal or plan, etc.

What is our natural tendency for tension in running? Too often, especially when faced with an adversity such as a steep hill or fast interval, it is to hurriedly smother the mixing board with our hands and mindlessly slam all of the faders up to their max setting. This is the quick fix-everything-including-the-kitchen-sink approach of immediately dialing up the tension levels in our body. I'll borrow a term from Spinal Tap fame to describe this default response and refer to it as Turning it all up to 11.

Just as the result of sliding all mixing board faders to their max setting in a music concert is an unpleasant distortion of sound that drowns out the nuances and subtleties of music, the result in our bodies when running is that we lock ourselves down, prevent efficient technique execution, and prevent our ability to reach flow. The next time you encounter a hill or start an interval run, ask yourself if you are moving all tension sliders "up to 11." If so, pull them back to zero and employ the artistry of a sound engineer to increase only the faders that are *absolutely necessary* up to the level where they produce the sound you are looking for, but nothing more.

Keep your tension level as low as possible, at MED, when running up and down hills. Here are three triggers to help you quickly reach MED when running:

- Relax your shoulders and gently pull your shoulder blades together, away from your ears, down and toward your spine. Your shoulders should move and rest in a downward direction, not rising upward toward your ears under tension.
- Relax your jaw and soften your facial expression.
- Shake your hands in the air, leaving as little tension as possible in them. Think of shaking off any stress in your day, right through your fingertips, and then breathe a fresh breath of air to charge your body with new strength and power.

5. Mastering Terrain

The following terrain types require some special considerations to ensure your optimal performance.

Soft Sand: minimize impact and distribute weight over as much foot surface area as possible (starting with forefoot impact), and master efficient technique (Pose Method®). Thinking of spinning through the sand (like on a mountain bike) instead of bounding and pushing through it. Orient your body to run vertically through the sand (pulling your feet up instead of kicking them forward) rather than horizontally (digging in and pushing off). The same applies for snow and ice hill running, in addition to some equipment considerations, such as using lightweight runner's crampons.

Pavement: downhill running on pavement requires maximum shock absorption through soft tissue, not your joints. Knees bent, relaxed body (at MED), slow your pace if you are not able to maintain a low impact,

Downhill on sand

Downhill on pavement

high cadence descent speed. Aim to be springy by bending your knees and lowering your center of gravity. And pull your feet off the ground quickly!

Rocky, loose, or otherwise technical trails: think like a downhill skier. Stay in a bent-knee athletic stance and focus on moving through a line of many steps, not moving from step to step. Assume that every time your foot touches the ground, the surface will not be stable. Rocks will move, and that gravel pile will slide, but your body will continue along the line you've painted in your mind. Accept the micro movements under your feet instead of fighting them. By keeping your center-of-gravity low and not fully weighting each foot strike in an unbalanced manner, you will be able to endure foot strikes on moving, unstable ground.

Downhill on trails

Equipment

For those times when running on hills takes you onto trails and/or into challenging weather conditions, there are several equipment considerations that are important to get right.

Shoes: While minimalist shoes are excellent for aiding proprioception, grip is a key factor in hill running. For years, I tested a wide range of shoes in hilly and mountainous terrain in Switzerland and found that poor grip, even in shoes designed and sold as trail running shoes, absolutely destroys confidence

and performance in both up and downhill running. Buy a shoe with reviews that clearly demonstrate positive experiences with grip in the terrain you plan to run in. It is more than simply how the cleats and lugs appear on the shoe. More important is the rubber compound. I love nothing more than fast downhill descent in wet technical terrain, but I've slipped and fallen countless times in what looked like aggressive, high tech trail running shoes, and the result was running in this terrain much slower than I wished. With a change in footwear though, I was able to stick where I wanted to stick, do a controlled slide in very slippery terrain, and ultimately run the pace I wanted to run.

Salomon Snowcross Shoes

Crampons or spikes: In snowy and icy conditions, you need either removable crampons or ice spikes built into the shoes. I've trained in both, and I prefer crampons over spikes. This is simply because I live and train most often in the winter in terrain with changing conditions versus a consistent snow or ice surface. For example, I may start a long run on dry pavement for a couple kilometers, then move to a trail covered in soft snow, before climbing to a hard-packed snow and ice-covered trail. The ability to put the crampons on and take them off makes me adaptable to changing conditions.

If your entire run is in consistent winter terrain (especially hard-packed snow and/or ice), then built-in spikes may serve you best. As for crampon selection, I'm a big fan of Kahtoola Microspikes and similar designs. In short, you want a very flexible crampon that in no way negatively impacts your foot movement and technique patterns, but that does not come off easily. I ran two winter seasons in Switzerland with lesser quality crampons that often flew off during long runs, leaving me to backtrack and go on crampon searches a frustrating number of times.

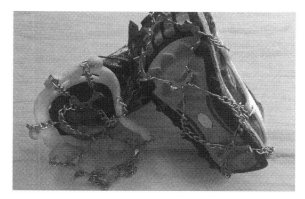

Kahtoola Microspikes

Trekking Poles: Trekking poles are often used in ultra marathons, especially in the Alps, where the terrain can be very steep. Their usage is a matter of personal preference. Poles are used when the terrain is sufficiently steep that it is more efficient to speed hike than to run, and the poles are used to aid speed hiking performance and share the workload with your upper body muscles. Poles are also useful in redistributing shock when downhill running.

The main consideration with poles is practicing with them to develop and instill technique patterns to draw on when racing, keeping the weight as light as possible, and deciding how to handle the poles when you don't need them. I raced the 166KM Ultra Trail du Mont Blanc (UTMB) with poles and chose to use the lightest possible version, one-piece (non-collapsible) carbon fiber. This saved weight, but meant that I had to keep the poles out at all times, instead of affixing them to my pack. For an extremely mountainous race such as UTMB and the hilly training runs I did for it, this made sense, as I incorporated the poles in nearly the entire course and learned to run with them at my sides with ease on flat terrain.

If your terrain varies from steep climbs to rolling hills to long valleys, you may appreciate the packability of collapsible poles. When you start training with poles, remember to keep the cadence high, even when walking. Your arm cadence will of course match your foot cadence, but thinking in terms of quickly moving arms and feet will help you maintain an efficient cadence on the climbs. It will also help you avoid the climb turning into a death-march, with a slow pace and a hunched-over body.

Racing the Ultra Trail du Mont Blanc with Trekking Poles

Closing Thoughts

Hill Running Technique involves a key set of skills to learn, practice, and master. Learning these skills is your ticket to surviving hill running, that is, getting through it so that you can continue to your destination. To reach your full potential as a hill runner though, to truly <u>thrive</u>, you must also master the crucial mental game, as it can undermine even the most powerful set of physical skills and talent! Let's move on to that topic now.

2. Hill Running Mind Hacks

It's all in your head

A strong mindset and toolkit of mental toughness skills makes a massive impact on your ability to **thrive** in the hills. Training your mind to perform in the hills is just as important as training your body, yet it is one area that many runners overlook, and in doing so, never fully realize their true potential.

In this chapter, I share powerful hill running mental tools, starting with the concept that there is immense power in convincing yourself that hills are not as different from flat terrain as you may have always thought!

I refer to these tools as Mind Hacks, in that they are designed to hack or alter your *status quo* state and in doing so, help you achieve a higher level of performance. Too often that status quo state is a distracted mind or worse, a mind that allows your Inner Critic too much power to negatively influence your performance, hindering your willingness to push through discomfort.

Let's explore eight key mental techniques that will transform your hill running performance:

Mind Hack 1: Close your eyes

Intention: Make the hill less sleep by recalibrating your mind and resetting your perception.

Instructions: Practice running up hill with your eyes closed or covered. Discover the change in perception and then remember this feeling any time you encounter a hill in your running. Use this technique with a sighted "guide" or practice it solo in safe terrain for short periods of time. You can engage this mind hack as well in long distance hilly running, such as in ultra marathons and trail runs, when you are literally running up mountains and need to remind yourself that the challenge is not as daunting as your eyes are suggesting.

Notes & Additional Insights: This technique sounds alarm bells for many runners. *What?! Run with your eyes closed?* Yes--but only in a safe setting, of course. To start with this technique, run in an obstacle-free open space with a friend guiding you by your arm

and with your eyes closed. Practice in flat terrain until you are comfortable running blind and are able to focus your senses on feeling your efficient technique and movement, without worrying about falling or bumping into something. If it makes you nervous to run with your eyes closed, then I encourage you to stick with it and keep practicing, as a newfound strength awaits when you tackle your fears head-on. When running uphill blind, focus on maintaining MED, staying in an upright body position with relaxed shoulders, and pulling your feet.

Once you are comfortable in flat terrain, shift to a hill that you have run before. Run up the hill with your sighted escort and have them stop you at the top. When you open your eyes at the top, you will be surprised at how "flat" the hill felt!

You also can practice this technique alone in the appropriate terrain (wide open, grass hills, parks, etc.), closing your eyes for a duration that your pre-run visual scan shows you is free from obstacles. I often use this technique on long mountain running climbs and close my eyes for just a handful of steps, enough time to "remind" my mind that the terrain is not as steep as I falsely perceive it to be.

When you build some experience blind running on hills, you will quickly learn that hill running has much more in common with <u>flat</u> running than it does with vertical rock climbing!

Mind Hack 2: Change your Pavlovian response

Intention: Change your perception: the hill is the reward, not the punishment.

Instructions: Every time you see a hill, react with an immediate "YES!" If you don't feel it, fake it. Then, smile.

Notes & Additional Insights: In addition to re-training your mind that hills aren't the menacing beast you once thought they were, you will also benefit from changing your Pavlovian response to hills. Remember the Pavlov's Dogs experiment, where the dogs responded to a stimulus (bell) by salivating in expectation of a reward (food)? This is a conditioned stimulus--the dogs were conditioned to respond to the bell with their expectation that it is associated with food.

The same applies to your conditioned response to hills. If your response to seeing a hill is to think, "OH NO!!" you will activate your Inner Critic. You will have painted the hill as a punishment and your Inner Critic—the preeminent expert at unraveling you— will convince you that the hill is much harder, and your abilities much less, than reality. If, on the other hand, you condition yourself to think, "YES, BRING IT ON!" when you see a hill, you will create a link between the hill and thriving under adversity. So, it's "Yes!", not "Oh no!" when you see hills. It doesn't matter whether or not you are truly happy and excited to see a hill. If you are not, then fake it.

When I coach at military-oriented training events, I instruct athletes to enthusiastically shout "Hooyah Hill!" or "Hooyah Stairs!" every time they see hills and stairs in their path. When you condition yourself to this response, you build a new strength to empower yourself with at first sight of these challenges. Do this 100 times and your natural reaction will become an enthusiastic, energized response and this will empower you to perform at a higher level on the hills.

Lastly, smile or just laugh at the hill. This serves as an immediate redirection of any negativity associated with the hill. While seemingly too-simple-to-be-true, smiles and laughter are time-tested tools for dealing with adversity. Don't miss the chance to pick this low-hanging fruit: smile on your next climb!

Mind Hack 3: Use Mantras

Intention: Positively focus your mind by repeating a mantra.

Instructions: Mantras are words or short phrases that convey a message and are often repeated internally or out loud to create a change in state. Create a library of mantras that resonate with you. Practice your top 3-5 most effective mantras and use them when you need a boost on a hill run. Repeat the mantra over and over in your mind or out loud.

Notes & Additional Insights: I have a collection of mantras that work for me, and in general they differ based on the duration of the climb and the intensity I'm seeking. Rarely when I use a mantra, do I "feel" it at first. If I were feeling 100% mentally strong, I wouldn't need a Mind Hack in that moment. I'm using it to get up to 100% of peak performance.

For long climbs, my go-to mantra is *Happy-Happy-Happy-Climb-Climb-Climb*. Am I truly happy when repeating this? Often not, especially at first chant! Yes, my teeth are sometimes clenched at the first Happy! But the mantra prompts a shift in my mindset, quietens my Inner Critic, and only a slight mind shift can make a huge impact in performance. Another long duration mantra I favor is, "This is why you're here."

Mantras are a very personal tool. Sometimes, we need aggressive mantras, such as:

- Own it!
- Get it DONE!
- GO NOW!
- Strong!
- Courage!
- Fight!
- Pain is temporary, pride is eternal

Other times, we need mantras that keep us calm and closer to MED, such as:

- Easy Hill
- Float, Fly, Free
- Breathe
- I got this
- Easy Day
- Be the wind

Experiment with many different mantras and then select what works for you.

Intention: Create and internalize a mental high performance state that you will later experience with your body.

Instructions: Create imagery in your mind of you succeeding on a hill run. Replay that imagery frequently until you program your brain to accept this as your only possible reality. Visualize yourself running hills with strength, speed, and a positive attitude. See yourself in your mind's eye as if you are a drone hovering overhead and also from the perspective of your eyes.

Notes & Additional Insights: Visualization is another low hanging fruit of mind hacks. It isn't always easy, and it takes practice, but it is an essential tool for developing mental strength and priming your neural pathways. In a visualization, you will see yourself as thriving with the highest level of performance you can imagine. This is an especially useful technique when training for a race with a notable climb, such as that special hill late in a marathon, or mountain passes in a trail ultra marathon. Following the intention of a visualization practice, you will live the reality you create in your mind, so create a highlight reel of your performance BEFORE the race. Then, once you find yourself on that climb DURING the race, you will be on familiar, high performance territory.

To prepare for visualization practices, write out the script you want to see. It is especially effective to see yourself encountering and overcoming adversities. Script it, and then close your eyes and watch the film you have created. Repeat it in your mind regularly.

Using the practice of Guided Visualizations, where you follow the mental imagery offered by someone else, is another useful tool. I really enjoy preparing Guided Visualization sessions for the athletes I coach and listening to other Guided Visualizations to help me get to desired mind states for mental or physical performance.

Mind Hack 5: Run through the summit

Intention: Move the prize and train yourself to run <u>through</u> the summit, not just to it. This technique makes you stronger when dealing with false summits.

Instructions: Run at least 10 steps beyond the first available stopping point at the top of every hill.

Notes & Additional Insights: Train yourself to run through the summit, instead of immediately stopping at the top of every hill. Too often, runners focus on the top to such extent that they are disappointed with every false summit. These runners are training themselves to essentially quit at the first available opportunity. This approach magnifies the severity of every hill. Don't give the hill the power—reward yourself fully with the power you own, the power you have cultivated. By running even a short distance beyond the top, you take power over the hill.

Mind Hack 6: Other People

Intention: Use the power of Other People to get more from yourself. Do this by racing, cheering, or honoring them.

Instructions: Use this tool on three levels

- **Level 1:** Race Someone—Identify a runner to catch, pass, and/or lead
- **Level 2:** Cheer Someone—Redirect your energy support another runner
- **Level 3:** Honor Someone—Tap into emotional power by dedicating your run to someone special

Each level can be activated with other runners present or as an in-flight visualization.

In my experience, Honor is the most powerful tool and works well in clutch moments, such as major adversities and late in a race.

Notes & Additional Insights: On a warm spring evening at the base of Zurich's scenic Uetliberg mountain, I assembled a group of runners. After warming up and working on some technique drills I led the group up a steep hill, pointing out the starting and ending points for a series of upcoming intervals.

We ran back down the hill to the start and I counted them down for their first hill interval.

3, 2, 1 Go! And off they went. They returned, and I sent them off again for their 2nd hill interval. For both of these intervals, I had given them little guidance other than a coach's direct and simple, "run fast up that hill." There was a mix of enthusiasm, groaning and pain faces during the interval. Their running was decent, but far from their best.

When I had them all back together again at the start line, I introduced them to the Other People tool.

Other People operates on 3 levels. I introduced the first level by challenging them to pick someone in the group to race up the hill. Their mission was to race this person, and if they passed them, to chase down the next person. The lead runner's mission was to stay in the lead. The results showed a marked improvement for the whole group over their first two attempts. Heads were held higher, and the paces quicker. I could instantly feel the group's spirits lift and intimidation of the hill fade. In the quick post-interval debrief, they mentioned feeling a spark of energy from the sudden competitive focus, especially for those not often competitively driven.

Now, on to Level 2. I tasked them with focusing entirely on cheering any runner around them, in front, behind, beside — it didn't matter. My instructions: just pick someone and cheer them. I launched them into the interval and watched with a smile as they not only stormed the hill but did so with great energy being poured into each other, especially in the later stages where the incline increased along with their fatigue. We debriefed back at the start line, and the runners shared how they momentarily forgot about their pain when they were encouraging someone else. This was precisely the intention, and I was happy to see them experience it firsthand.

To prepare for Level 3, I handed them each a paper and pen and asked them to close their eyes and take three deep breaths. Then, I asked that they focus their mind and soul on someone who holds an extremely high value in their lives, perhaps a parent, child, partner or friend. Following some quiet reflection time, I asked that they write down the name of this person on their paper, and then asked them to fold the paper and place it in their palm. Their mission was to run up the hill with every movement and breath serving as a passionate reflection of the honor they feel for the person whose name was being held in their palm.

Everything they would do from the moment I said *GO!* until the moment they topped the hill was to be in this person's honor.

There was an immediate change in the atmosphere at this moment. No one said a word. Their eyes said it all. We had just created a sacred space, a small group all focusing on someone special to them and about to offer a physical performance in their honor. Years later, I still get goose bumps when I recall this moment — actually, I get them every time I coach this exercise to this day.

When they received the call to start, they soared away from the start line. I saw a level of performance from each and every runner that I had never seen before. That peak performance state, which is inside of each one of us, surfaced in a profound way in this group. It was such a heightened and emotional state that there was very little conversation on the way back down the hill. The group was numb from the experience. A few had selected such a dear person to them that they cried during the interval. Others were emotional afterward. We went on an easy cool down run to allow everyone to reach a calm state and to process what they had just experienced. It was an inspiring night of training.

Level 1, racing someone, is effective at tapping into one's competitive spirit and is an effective tool at just about any stage of a run. Level 2, cheering someone, is useful especially when you are suffering in a run and want to get your mind off of your suffering (because you know now that continuing to dwell on it will not make the suffering or adversity vanish).

The final level, honoring someone, is the most special — it is rocket fuel. Rocket fuel is extremely powerful, but it is also volatile, expensive, and in limited supply. So, use this level wisely and conservatively for those key moments when you need to dig deep. Level 3 works well in visualizations, like the visualization I shared from the Marathon des Sables when I "saw" my closest friends and family members running with me in the desert. It also works well when writing names on slips of paper and looking at the names at different pre-planned stages of a race. I can't tell you how many marathons I've run where I focused the last few kilometers on honoring my mom or dad!

Mind Hack 7: Focal Points

Intention: Control your vision and points of focus

Instructions: Select one of the three vision techniques below:

- **Single Point Focus:** Pick any object in your sight and focus as intently as possible on that object. Focus so hard that everything else fades away, out of focus. This tool is especially useful in hill running, where you can select as your target a tree or plant at the top of the hill, or simply on the path in front of you. This tool combines well with the BLUE *Colors* tool, coming up later in this section.
- **Wide Scan:** Expand your vision as wide as possible. Think in terms of using the maximum power of your peripheral vision, while keeping your gaze soft. This combines well with the GREEN *Colors* tool, coming up later in this section.
- **High Speed Tunnel:** Create tunnel vision, but with a soft focus toward the end of the tunnel instead of a strong, narrow focus. Allow the sides to rush by quickly in a blur, just like you're in a train speeding through a tunnel.

Notes & Additional Insights: A single point of focus works well when you need to focus your concentration or redirect any negativity in your mind. As an energizing focus, it is very effective in short intervals and when you need to redirect your brain from overload mode into a problem-solving mode. It's also a useful tool in reinforcing micro goals, such as running hard just to the next tree, the next rock, or the next switchback on the trail.

A wide scanning focus is effective for pulling in new energy and inputs from your environment. It is a calming focus, and one that reminds you that you are part of the world around you. It is effective in tempo runs, which are longer and at a lower intensity level than interval runs, thus requiring a sustained level of intensity, which the wide scan fosters.

The high-speed tunnel technique supports detaching mind and body to endure a higher pain threshold. Keeping the gaze soft at the end of the tunnel serves as a calming reminder, allowing the tunnel itself to support your concentration, without a specific end point to focus on. It is also a good tool to use when you need to let go of something that isn't serving you in a run, or when you need to quickly shut down your Inner Critic.

For example, we have a very long tunnel in Switzerland that goes under the Alps — the Gotthard Tunnel. It is known as the magic weather tunnel, because it often seems that separate seasons are occurring on both sides of the tunnel. Winter rages and lingers on the North side, while spring arrives early and often on the South side.

When using the high-speed tunnel technique, I often think of the magic weather tunnel. When you are in it, that snow storm which was just hammering you suddenly vanishes. In the tunnel there is no weather, and for a good fifteen minutes, no sign of the other end. You simply drive straight ahead with faith that you'll eventually exit the mountain. In running, this equates to going to a safe, calm mind space when you escape into the tunnel, thus removing weather from the equation. While in the tunnel, you are free to simply run, with no expectations. Once on the other side, you will enter a different season, sometimes even with sunshine and warm temperatures.

This tool is helpful when running in a lane on the track during intervals and during races.

Mind Hack 8: Color Mapping

Intention: Associate colors with energy and concepts and draw from those colors when you see them on your hill run.

Instructions: Assign a color or colors to moments of your run where you need additional support. Use the color mappings below, or create your own. You can also integrate colors with visual focus techniques. Use this tool to train your powers of observation and awareness.

Green
- Energy that pulls you forward and supercharges your system
- Plants / trees giving off oxygen, visualize breathing 100% pure Oxygen
- Wide scan focus
- With each inhalation, allow your eyes to relax and see WIDE angle
- Allow the green to enter and charge the body.

Red / Orange
- Energy that PUSHES you forward like solar waves arriving on your back
- Warm energy
- With each exhalation, allow your eyes to focus on a single point and feel the red energy push you forward

Blue

- Energy like a blue laser or refreshingly cool blue lake
- Cooling energy with wide scan focus
- Warming energy with narrow, laser beam focus
- With each inhale, the blue intensifies, along with its associated concepts

White

- Energy that envelopes and calms you
- Peace, stillness, cerebral
- Inhalation: white energy descends from clouds and wraps you up in peace and calm

Brown

- Energy that pulls you forward and faster
- Earth – gravity
- Falling toward the earth, as it spins
- Exhalation: surrender, and gravity does the work for you

Mixed Colors

- Energy pulsations, waves or sparks
- Like wildflowers or twinkling stars
- Runs up and down the spine, as a quick charge or boost, tapping into each color briefly and making you instantly more alert

Background: I have a love-hate relationship with a mile-long trail run hill next to my home. It is one of my least favorite and most favorite benchmark runs. Here is how I experience it using this mind hack:

Two minutes in, and my heart rate is elevated such that I'm dancing the edge of my lactate threshold. My awareness kicks in and determines that I'm not at MED. I address it with a tension dumper and then bring my attention to the green undergrowth in the forest. With each inhalation, I feel the extra oxygen and an associated boost in power. I look up

and see the white of a cloud, so on the exhalations I feel the peace of the color white float down and envelope me. Inhale energy-green — exhale peace-white. Four minutes in, and I pass a red park bench. Like waves of solar energy, I feel red pushing at my back, pushing me up the hill. Now at the 6-minute mark, I need a new fuel and notice a descending runner wearing a blue shirt. I focus on blue, which I associate with laser focus. I narrow my focus to a small field of view just ahead and up, and I keep charging for that circle. At the crux of the climb, I notice some spring wild flowers popping up. I link these with little sparks of energy running up and down my spine. I feel this energy, straighten my posture and ride this last energy wave to the finish.

I love using this tool on a track as well. The running track near my home is red with green grass in the infield. During intervals, I open my eyes wide to draw in the green energy of the grass as I inhale, narrow my gaze to the next corner and feel the red surface under my feet rise to push my back as I exhale. I see the white lines dividing the lanes and feel an inner calmness. I draw from the blue sky to feel cooling energy that refreshes my overheating legs. These visualizations happen in a matter of seconds, but the impact is profound. It is a simple, yet powerful technique.

Increasing your awareness of your environment will build a stronger general awareness foundation, thus a stronger foundation for entering heightened performance states such as the flow state. On your next run, simply notice how many colors you see, in what amounts and frequency. Really tune in your awareness. Even in winter when brown may seem predominant, there are typically a wide range of colors available when you really open your eyes and enter a hyper-aware state. Some of my most powerful color experiences have occurred in the desert or snowy mountains because the colors that do appear really pop.

These color inputs are freely available to you. You can assign any significance you want. Colors offer a target rich environment. The *Colors* tool doesn't have to be just for intervals. It is also available as a calming technique before, during, or after running, or simply anytime in your life. While there are always colors available for use in the environment, you may also choose to wear specific colors with helpful meaning attached, or associate a meaning to colors you are already drawn to, or to your favorite gear.

I like to include color in pre-race running visualizations, linking a specific color to a performance concept, and then using that color in my race gear.

Is it ok to walk the hills?

With this toolkit of mind hacks available, I would like to now cover a very important topic in hill running: walking.

First, the only one whose judgement matters on the topic of how you approach a hill or walking at any point during a run or race is YOU. It frustrates me as a coach to hear new runners describe how they "failed" in their first 5K race because they had to walk at some point. They covered the distance on their own, so that's not a failure in my book. Running is human-powered locomotion, moving from one place to another. So is walking. Elite race-walkers finish 20KM races (1.1 KM short of a half marathon) between 1.25 and 1.5 hours.[1] Average half marathon times for <u>runners</u> are roughly between 2 and 2.5 hours.[2] So, elite walkers are covering a half marathon by <u>walking</u> significantly faster than average runners run that same distance.

Does that mean that average runners or any level of racewalkers are "failing" in their race efforts? No!

The concept of "not walking" in a run can be a useful motivator, so if it helps you push harder and get more performance out of yourself, then use it. I've seen the dark side of this concept though, and it is largely about losing control of one's ego. I recall a mountain bike race I was in where I spent half an hour on a climb fighting like mad to pedal up a steep incline, refusing to get off my bike and walk. Ego on, impact neutral.

The whole time there was a guy in front of me

pushing his bike up the hill, at the exact same speed, but much lower intensity and frustration level than me. He was showing me that there was a smarter way to move on this part of the course, but I was a slow learner. I thought to myself, "There's no way I'm going to give in and succumb to the walk of shame." I wobbled and growled my way a bit further up the hill, veins on my forehead nearly bursting and a grumble of cursing in my head. Ego on, impact negative. I eventually let go of my ego and walked — smart choice. I caught and passed the "walker" and a few more wobbling, riding holdouts, recovered along the way, and rode the descent full of energy. I later scolded myself for not wising up and dropping my ego sooner. Lesson learned.

The same applies in running. Be smart — if walking and running are the same speed on a given terrain for you, walk. This is especially useful in trail races and ultra marathons. During that walk though, shift your intensity to your mental effort. Tap in to one of the mind hacks you've learned and build your mental fuel reserve for what is to come.

In addition, use the time to tend to your fueling and hydration needs, check your map if you're in that kind of race, and sort out any gear or clothing adjustments. I used walk breaks extensively in the Marathon des Sables, always tending to my hydration, nutrition or equipment during these very short recovery breaks. It was a challenge to let go of my ego to do each planned break in full, but it enabled me to pass dozens of runners late in each stage, faster runners who didn't give enough attention to maintaining their bodies early in the run.

And by all means, when you need to run a hill to reach your race goals, run it. And if you've got hills near home, train on them. They are good for the mind, body and soul! Remember to use an efficient technique when you're running uphill, upright posture (don't hunch your torso over at the waist) and quick feet.

Be a Hillseeker

I would like to close this chapter with a discussion of the HILLSEEKER mentality. I founded a company with this name and I actively encourage a hill seeking approach to life. This simple philosophy has made a huge difference in my life—I hope in some way it supports you as well, so I would like to share the philosophy behind it.

Why Hillseeker? Why not Mountain Finder? or Peak Bagger?

To me, hillseeking is a way of life -- a way of life that goes well beyond sport, beyond mountains, beyond rising ground, rising sand, or rising water.

Hillseeking is that moment when you see one faint trail pitch up a steep mountainside and another well-marked trail continue through the valley, and your heart flutters in excitement as you absolutely can't stand the thought of not checking out the trail up the mountain.

A Hillseeker gets excited at the thought of going up something -- less about standing on the top, but more about the thought and journey of trying to move upward through whatever challenges 'upward' may bring.

Hillseeking in the Swiss Alps

This is just a sports thing, right? No way. A Hillseeker feels a magnetic pull to that challenging project at the office or in the field -- the kind of project where uncertainty abounds, and the path to the summit is far from clear and likely treacherous in spots.

A Hillseeker is so incredibly alive at that moment that the uphill path is chosen and then flourishes as the challenging journey unfolds.

A Hillseeker is a 12-year old girl practicing backwards basketball shots over and over and refusing to give up until she unlocks the secret. Hillseeking is found in a group of 7-year old boys trying time and time again to ride up a steep mound of dirt at a construction site without falling off their bikes.

A Hillseeker is the 84-year old woman who encourages her 78-year old neighbor to walk up the path to the overlook on their Sunday morning stroll, and the 92-year old man who walks two hours every day around his hilly neighborhood. A Hillseeker is the 17-year old who decides to take AP Biology as an elective course. Hillseekers are also runners who decide to go for their first marathon, cyclists who go for their first big ride in the mountains, and of course mountaineers who long for the climb and lure of the peaks.

A Hillseeker embraces life for its challenges and feels overwhelming joy at those moments when the trail steepens.

Be a Hillseeker!

[1] https://en.wikipedia.org/wiki/Racewalking
[2] http://www.runningusa.org/index.cfm?fuseaction=news.details&ArticleId=333

3. Strength & Conditioning

To get the results you seek, you've got to do the work

Building a Strong Hill Running Body

There is a school of thought that to get good at running hills, or at least to endure it, you simply have to run hills a lot. This means living in hilly or mountainous terrain. It also means having the time to get to the hills for your training sessions even if you do live near them. If you live in the Rockies, the Appalachians, the Alps or other ranges and areas with undulating terrain, perhaps you've got all you need right at your doorstep. But many runners don't have the luxury, including the available time, to get out into this prized terrain. If this is you, then there are indeed smart ways to train your mind and body for hills without running on them daily.

I encourage you to apply the MED concept to your training. Think of training as a dose of something you are taking to effect a change, and your performance in the hills as the desired outcome. You are seeking just the right amount of that dose to make the desired outcome happen. Not enough, and the change won't happen. Too much, and you've just wasted time and energy in overdoing it. Getting the dose right has everything to do with being smart in how you build it. It's not a game of volume, but rather intelligent programming of your training approach based on your strengths, weaknesses, and needs.

In this chapter, I teach you how to train your body to adapt to the strength and conditioning

Box Step-ups: beard is optional

demands of hill running. I cover Strength Training both with and without equipment. In addition, I share some very important coaching guidance on conditioning and cross-training. The 10-week Training Program included in the Expanded Online Coaching edition of this book is built on this foundation. With that plan and this knowledge base, you'll be prepared to build future plans for yourself and to adapt your program based on your own needs.

Strength Training

I highly recommend that you include strength training in your overall program to improve your performance and durability when running on trails and in other challenging terrain conditions. Performance requires little explanation: less time required to cover a distance or less energy exuded to cover it in the same time.

Durability may not be quite as clear. By durability, I mean your ability to endure running on extremely challenging surfaces that are working their hardest to sprain your ankle, strain or tear ligaments in your knee, and inflame your tendons and joints to the point that you are not able to run. Durability comes from strength and is developed through training—not from luck. So, invest early in building durability and it will serve you well on race day!

General Strength Training Principles

Start with your core. This is your basis. If you had to choose only one strength training focus to improve your running, choose core training. Without a strong core, you will not be able to maintain efficient running form and you will sacrifice durability, which leaves you at risk of injury.

On top of a strong core, build lower body strength. To increase strength—particularly in your ankles, feet, legs, and core—train primarily with fundamental movement patterns, such as squats, lunges, pushing and dragging sleds, box step-ups, and jumping.

For pure strength development of your posterior chain (lower back, glutes, and hamstrings), nothing beats heavy weight, low rep squats and deadlifts with a barbell. It doesn't take much time in the gym to make a major impact on your strength and resulting durability in rough terrain.

For stamina development, train primarily with bodyweight functional movements, such as air squats, lunges, and burpees. Volume will be higher for building stamina than for raw strength development.

I highly recommend that start your investment in strength development well before race day. Your resilient, healthy and non-injured body will thank you!

Let's look now at specific exercises.

Bodyweight Strength Training for Hills

You can make significant gains in strength using nothing more than your own body, thus the "weight" you'll be lifting and moving is your own bodyweight. Below, I have outlined the key bodyweight movements to master. If you are new to these movements, nothing beats working in-person with a qualified trainer to ensure that your technique is correct. If you use improper technique, especially with high volume workouts, you risk injuring yourself. Visit Hillseeker.com for demo versions of these exercises.

Air Squats: Feet shoulder width, toes straight ahead or slightly pointing out. Keep your heels weighted as you reach your hips back and bend your knees. Go deep (hip crease below top of knee) and keep your back straight with your chest facing forward. Push your knees out (don't allow them to collapse inward).

Air Squats

Jump Squats: Initiate the same as with squats. As you near the top of the squat, spring upward into the air. Land softly and quietly.

Jump Squats

Wall Sits: Squat with your back to a wall. Keep your thighs parallel to the floor and back fully pressed against the wall. Make sure your lower back maintains wall contact and that your knees track over your toes. Keep your hands off of your legs. I recommend arms in front or holding a weight.

Wall Sits

Lunges: Step one leg forward, bend knees until back knee touches the ground. Don't go beyond vertical for the front shin (you may need to step further out in front than you think). You may do them in place (returning to the starting position after each lunge) or walking forwards or backwards.

Lunges

Jump Lunges: Initiate just like a Lunge. When you extend your legs to change sides, spring into the air. Land softly right into the next lunge.

Step-ups: Step up onto a box, bench, large rock, or other suitable object. Follow with the other leg and step tall at the top. Then, step back down. Variations include stepping from the side (lateral step-ups), varying the height, using weight, alternating or doing same-side only step-ups, and jumping instead of stepping (known as Box Jumps).

Box Step-ups

Box Jumps

Mountain Climbers: Start in push-up position. Jump your right foot forward until your right knee touches your right elbow. Your right heel should be on the ground. Then, jump your right foot back to the starting point as you jump your left foot forward.

Mountain Climbers

Burpees: Stand tall, hands to the ground, jump feet back to push-up position, lower body to the ground, initiate the start of a push-up, jump feet back up to the squat stance, stand-up and spring into the air. Hands to side or clap overhead. Make sure you open your hips at the top of each burpee. Regular Burpees involve five counts (1. hands to ground, 2. feet back, 3. down push-up, 4. roll torso up and jump feet to a squat, 5. jump up).

Ready Position   1. Hands to ground

2. Jump back to the top of a push-up

3. Lower to the ground

4. Jump to the bottom of a squat.

5. Spring into the air. Open your hips.

Note: *heels are on the ground, not elevated.*

Hillseeker Burpees: These are 8-count burpees. The difference is a full push-up is performed after Step 3 above. Then, a Mountain Climber on both sides is added after the UP part of the push-up.

Sit-ups: I highly recommend using an Ab-Mat for sit-ups, as it focuses the movement more on your core and less on your hip flexors. Bottoms of your feet together, knees out to the sides.

1. Hands to ground

2. Jump back to the top of a push-up

3. Jump back to the top of a push-up. Steps 1-3 are the same as regular burpees.

4. Push-up

5. Mountain Climber Left

6. Mountain Climber Right

7. Jump to the bottom of a squat.

Note: *heels are on the ground, not elevated.*

8. Spring into the air. Open your hips.

Sit-ups: I highly recommend using an Ab-Mat for sit-ups, as it focuses the movement more on your core and less on your hip flexors. Bottoms of your feet together, knees out to the sides.

Hollow Hold: Lie on your back with your legs straight and arms stretched out overhead. Lift your arms and legs so that both face straight up. Engage your core and press your lower back into the ground. Lower your arms and legs until your lower back starts to lift from the ground. Press your lower back into the ground and hold this position as your "Hollow" position.

Sit-ups

Hollow Hold

Flutter Kicks: Lie on your back. Place your hands under your hips, palms down flat or in fists. Lift your head up and look toward your feet, or keep it in a neutral position on the floor. Press your lower back into the ground and hold it there. Alternate lifting your legs, keeping them straight and pointing your toes.

Flutter Kicks

Supermans: Lie on your belly with your legs together and arms overhead. Lift your arms and legs up at the same time. Focus on reaching with your arms and legs (making yourself as long as possible) while lifting them up.

Supermans

Reverse Crunches: Lie on your back with knees bent, feet on the ground. Draw your knees toward your chest, engage your abs and lift your hips off the ground.

Leg Levers: Both legs together, lower back pressed into the ground. Raise and lower legs.

Leg Levers

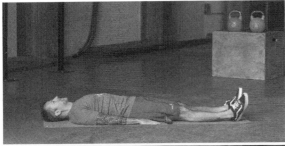

Reverse Crunches

Plank and Variations: Body stays straight as a board. Arm positions can vary from straight arms to weight on forearms. Plank walk-ups is a movement where you alternate between elbow plank and straight arm plank. Side plank is a 1-arm plank with weight either on forearm or hand and top hip facing straight up. Plank Toe Taps or Plank Leg raises involves alternate lifting of your legs either straight up or up and then tapping toe to heel.

Plank: snow is optional

Equipment-Based Strength Movements

If you want to take your strength training to the next level, then it's worth investing in a gym membership or building your own small garage gym. In a popular article on Hillseeker.com, I share my guidance on equipment to buy for a garage gym, including equipment specific to runner's needs. If you decide on joining a gym, then I recommend a functional training or CrossFit gym over a large franchise gym with fitness machines.

Below are the key strength training movements with equipment that I recommend you include in your program. In general, for strength development as a hill runner, I encourage you to focus on low rep sets (3-6 reps) with heavy weight. For stamina, the focus shifts to lower weight, higher volume sets.

Barbell Squats: Back Squats and Front Squats are the most useful squat styles for running-related strength. Back squats are performed with a barbell across the back of your shoulders, either in a high bar or low bar position. Front squats are performed with the barbell in front of your chest, elbows high and facing away from your chest, not down.

Back Squat top position

Back Squat bottom position

Front Squat top position

Front Squat bottom position

Kettlebell Goblet Squats: These squats are performed with a Kettlebell held at your chest. Keep your back straight and chest facing forward.

Kettlebell Goblet Squat

Deadlifts: Deadlifts target your posterior chain (glutes, hamstrings, lower back), all of which you need strength in to excel in the hills. Of all the strength exercises, Deadlifts are the most important to have your form checked by a qualified trainer. It's imperative to maintain a neutral spine position throughout this movement and to perform it in a way that activates your posterior chain, not incorrectly by squatting into the movement. You can deadlift many different kinds of objectives. For developing hill running strength, I recommend using a barbell or kettlebell. It's usually easier to get the kind of weight you need with a barbell (with weight plates), but there are some very heavy kettlebells on the market!

Deadlift setup position side view

Deadlift bottom position front view

Deadlift start position side view

Deadlift top position front view

Deadlift top position side view

Kettlebell Deadlift setup position

Kettlebell Deadlift start position

Kettlebell Deadlift top position

Kettlebell Swings: This movement is performed either 1- or 2-handed. I recommend the Russian Style Swing, where you swing the kettlebell up to shoulder height. Use your hips and knee extension to create the pendulum movement and send the kettlebell up. Maintain a neutral spine with your chest facing forward, not down.

Kettlebell Swing

Core Barbell or Ab Wheel Rollouts: With your knees on the ground, grasp a barbell or Ab Wheel and roll the barbell or wheel away from your knees. Maintain a neutral spine and tight core. Do not allow your back to sway and hips to sag down toward the floor.

TRX Training: There's so much you can do with this simple piece of equipment and your body weight, focusing on all parts of your body. My favorites for hill running strength development are single leg squats (holding the handles with your hands), lunges with one foot in the TRX, and Knees-in (both feet in straps, push-up position, draw feet to elbows).

Sandbag Training: You can make a DIY Sandbag on a budget and perform a lot of barbell and kettle-bell movements with it, including squats, weighted lunges, weighted box step-ups, and Russian Twists. It's also a great tool for creating fun combined work-outs, such as sprints and sandbag squats. Check out my DIY guide and workouts article on Hillseeker. com for more info.

Training under Load: Running with a Weight Vest or Weighted Rucksack is a good way to build strength and durability, when done smartly and in a progressive, safe way. Start light (3-5% of your body weight) and for short distances (no more than a few minutes at a time). Gradually add weight and duration, but don't rush this. Training under load is particularly useful when speed-hiking steep hills. You can always carry water weight, dump it at the top, and run down unweighted.

Training with a weight vest and dragging two tires, on one of my favorite local hills

Agility Training

I also encourage you to train with agility exercises, such as ladder drills, lateral hops, and footwork drills found in ball sport training, especially for soccer and American football. This is useful for developing coordination skills, as well as strengthening your ankles for trail running.

Conditioning & Cross Training

On top of your strength base, we layer on conditioning work, both specific to hill running and in general support of your cardiovascular fitness. Incorporated into the high-level plans that I design for runners and present in the 10-Week Plan I created for the Expanded Online Coaching edition are a mix of run types:

- **Intervals:** high intensity effort, from very short sprints up to about 10 minutes. Favorites include Tabata (8x20sec sprint, 10sec rest), Fartlek (spontaneously selected targets), and 800-meter repeats.
- **Tempo:** lactate and anaerobic threshold training, at an intensity level lower than intervals and near that of a hard 5KM or 10KM run, depending on the runner's background, fitness and objectives. Duration can be from 10 minutes to over an hour.
- **Adventure:** mission, game or play-focused, at a variety of intensity levels and often incorporating functional training, novelty, and adventure.
- **Hills (of course!):** uphill or downhill, incorporating other run types, as well as skipping. Downhill training is an important and oft-overlooked tool for increasing speed on any terrain.
- **Speed Hiking / Power Walking:** While technically not a run type, this is a very important training tool for performance in the hills. Intensity varies from recovery pace (easy) to full speed hiking intervals.
- **Load:** running with weight (rucksack, weight vest) or dragging a tire.
- **Yin:** zero active technology utilization, zero time goals, focuses on awareness and experience
- **Easy / Long:** low to moderate intensity, steady effort. Includes active recovery runs as well as long runs.
- **Benchmarks:** Test runs, designed to simulate the competition setting as much as possible.

Each run type is important in creating a physiological and/or mindset adaptation in the runner, as well as a spark for their continued motivation and enthusiasm. When incorporated into a high-level plan, some of these run types are planned in progressions (such as long runs and 800-meter intervals). Others are incorporated with variation and spontaneity (such as Fartlek intervals and Adventure runs).

Cross-training

Cross-training is an important tool for injury prevention, variety, and maintaining your running fitness when, for any reason, you are not able to run (travel, injury, tapering, etc.). My top cross-training activities are as follows:

- **Skipping Rope:** Rope-skipping reinforces proper foot pull in running, while also offering an excellent conditioning stimulus. It's also very portable.
- **Rowing:** One of my favorite training tools during the winter is a Concept 2 rower. Rowing is one of the most effective cross training stand-ins for running and useful for any duration you would run, from short high-power intervals to tempo training, to long endurance sessions.
- **Cycling:** Indoor Cycling (such as a spinning class or on an Assault Air Bike) or riding outside.
- **Other Endurance Sports:** Swimming, XC Skiing, Hiking

Mobility

Integrating yoga into your life aids greatly in developing flexibility, body awareness, and a focused mind. Mobility and flexibility are key components to reaching peak performance states, as a supple body will support a supple mind, and vice versa. As a practitioner of yoga for 20 years and a qualified yoga teacher, I believe in the value of yoga as an integrated system to provide a solid foundation for all pursuits, athletic and otherwise. I practice some form of yoga daily and encourage my clients to integrate yoga even at the most minor level in their lives. I find it especially important to address the soreness, and impact of high intensity training, especially speed work.

Closing Thoughts

The best meals are prepared with quality ingredients brought together in the right combinations, in the right amounts, at the right time, with the right intention and care. The same applies to successful training that is directed at creating an improvement in your performance. The exercises and activities in this chapter have great potential to improve your hill running performance when you do them with proper form and in effective combinations and frequency

As just like with meals, it never hurts to have good friends around while eating and/or training!

4. Hill Training Library

This chapter includes 30 hill training sessions that span a range of training modes, settings, targets, and movement patterns. There is enough variety in this set of workouts to keep you inspired and building greater fitness for quite some time! You will find uphill and downhill running, skipping, integrated functional training, stairs workouts, games, and more. These sessions also provide you with sufficient inspiration and training ideas to build an unlimited set of additional hill training sessions to suit your environment, needs, and preferences. Each session is called a WOD, which is short for Workout of the Day.

If you are already following a training plan to prepare for a specific event, such as running a marathon, then I suggest that you incorporate at least one of these hill running sessions per week into your training plan, more if you are preparing for a mountainous race. Choose sessions that help you train your weaknesses and areas of your strength and conditioning that you find the most challenging.

For those runners looking for a full immersion into improving Hill Running performance, the Expanded Online Coaching version offers a 10-Week Training Plan. This plan uses these Hill Training sessions in a structured manner, while adding Mind Training and Strength and Conditioning work.

Hill WOD 1

Type: Short intervals

Instructions
- Down the Ladder: Run UPHILL as fast as you can for each of the following intervals: 100sec, 90sec, 80sec, 70sec, 60 ... to 10sec.
- Increase your pace with each interval.
- Rest exactly 90sec in between each. Spice it up by including a 30sec squat hold during each 90sec break.

Notes
- Make sure to include a sufficient warm-up and cool-down.
- Focus on relaxed shoulders and hands, as well as a high cadence and up right body position.

Hill WOD 2

Type: Combo, medium intervals

Instructions
- 5min HARD uphill
- 30 squats
- 5min EASY running or walking
- 5min HARD uphill
- 30 squats
- 5min EASY running or walking
- 2min SPRINT uphill
- 30 squats

Notes
Focus on keeping your shoulders super relaxed during the intervals. You'll likely be tempted to become overly tense, which will wreck your efficiency. Stay calm in mind and body and your performance will improve!

- Make sure to include a sufficient warm-up and cool-down, and do a few warm-up squats before you begin the workout.
- Stand with your feet at shoulder-width, initiate the movement by driving your hips backward maintaining a vertical upper body position throughout the movement, and keep your knees tracking out, directly over your toes.
- Go for it with intensity and maintain excellent squat form. Have fun!

Hill WOD 3

Type: Stairs, Game, Adventure

Get some on the stairs! This is a fun one that will zap your legs. Go for it!

Instructions
20-min AMSAP (As many steps as possible)

Your objective is to run up as many steps as possible, following the game below. Recovery is on the descent. If you don't have a long enough set of stairs to link together 25, 50 or 100 steps, just repeat whatever you have (including a single step) at high intensity until the target number is met. Then rest briefly.

Game
Roll a dice twice.

Roll 1:
- 1 or 2: single steps
- 2 or 3: double steps
- 5 or 6: wall sit or squat hold

Roll 2:
- 1 or 2: 25 steps
- 2 or 3: 50 steps
- 5 or 6: 100 steps

After each run or wall sit, note what you completed and roll again. Keep this up until 20 minutes is up. If your first roll of any round is a 5 or 6, that's a wall sit. Roll again and refer the Roll 2 - Steps table. The number of steps equals your wall sit in seconds. For example, a 3 or 4 on the 2nd roll is 50 seconds in a wall sit. A 5 or 6 is 100 seconds.

Tracking Your Score and Remembering the System

Write out a simple tracking sheet, like the one pictured here. When I first did this workout, I simply brought a handful of coins and some colored tabs. Each time I finished an interval, I dropped a coin into the appropriate quadrant. For wall sits, I dropped in a colored tab. Do the math after it's all over. Your FINAL score is the number of steps plus seconds in a wall sit, including the bonus round (see below).

Bonus Round

When 20 minutes is up, total your wall sit time. Take half of that number (in seconds) and this is your bonus round. After a 2-min rest, you may continue to roll the dice and play the game until this extra time expires or do a wall sit for this time or a combo. Add your steps and/or wall sit seconds to your score.

Wall Sits

How to do a wall sit: back against wall, legs at parallel in a squat position. Hold it!

Hill WOD 4

Type: Stairs, Game, Adventure

Instructions

- 3 Rounds of an 8-min AMRAP (As many rounds as possible).
- Find the steepest, meanest hill you can for this one, one that takes 1-2min to reach the top or a designated turnaround spot. If you don't have steep hills, then wear a weight vest or weighted backpack and run on any incline you can find. If you don't have ANY hills at all, then use stairs or simply a box to step up onto over and over.
- Run up as many times as possible in 8 minutes. Your time running down the hill is included in the 8min interval. Partial distance up counts as well.
- Rest 1-2 min in between each 8min round.

Notes

- Aim to improve your performance each round. Push yourself!
- Practice setting micro-goals (run to the next switchback, signpost or tree).
- Stay positive.
- Upright body, quick foot pulls

Inspired by Greek mythology and the story of Sisyphus, this hill training session is a TOUGH one for the mind and body! The story goes that Sisyphus was a king who got himself into trouble, a lot of trouble. Zeus had enough and punished Sisyphus to push an enormous boulder up a steep hill. Right before Sisyphus reached the top, Zeus sent the boulder back to the bottom, again and again. Sisyphus' resulting punishment was to push the boulder to the top of the hill an infinite number of times. I know what you're thinking, sounds like a great workout, right?!

Keep this gem in mind as you take on this workout, "Albert Camus, in his 1942 essay The Myth of Sisyphus, saw Sisyphus as personifying the absurdity of human life, but Camus concludes "one must imagine Sisyphus happy" as "The struggle itself towards the heights is enough to fill a man's heart." (source: Wikipedia)

Hill WOD 5

Type: Short, Mantra, Tabata

Instructions
4 rounds, all intervals 20sec, rest breaks vary.

All on a steep hill, set of stairs or treadmill on hill setting

- Round 1: 8x20 sec sprint with 10sec rest breaks (standard Tabata)
- 2min rest
- Round 2: 6x20 sec sprint with 20sec rest breaks
- 2min rest
- Round 3: 4x20 sec sprint with 40sec rest breaks
- 2min rest
- Round 4: 2x20 sec sprint with 60sec rest breaks

Notes
- Pick a different mantra to use for each round. Focus on that mantra for each of the 20sec intervals in that round. Plan these in advance and use them to serve as a boost in the WOD. I used the following mantras when I tested this workout: easy spin, strong, smile, fly.
- Technique reminders: upright body, quick foot pulls

Hill WOD 6

Type: Short

Instructions

3-4 rounds

All on a steep hill, set of stairs, treadmill on hill setting. All uphill.

- 30-sec sprint Section A
- 1min rest
- 30-sec sprint Section B
- 1min rest
- 1min sprint Sections A+B
- 2min rest

Notes

It works well on a two-part climb, but it is possible on a single short hill or set of stairs, or even with box step-ups. The section letters are simply whatever course you select for each of the two parts. It can be the first half of a hill and the second half.

Hill WOD 7

Type: Skipping, Combo

This one is a leg BURNER! The combination of high skips performing uphill, a long set of walking lunges and squats as "recovery" brings the magic in this session.

Instructions

- All on a steep hill or whatever terrain you have to work with. Set a start line and a 24-minute countdown timer.
- Ten 2-count high skips
- Backwards lunge walk to the start line
- Eight 2-count high skips
- Backwards lunge walk to the start line
- 8 squats
- Continue the pattern with 6, 4, 2 reps. After 2 reps continue the pattern with 4, 6, 8, 10. Keep adding two reps until the 24-minute clock expires.

BONUS 1: 100 downhill 2-count walking lunges immediately after the 24-min timer expires. Take BIG steps for each lunge.

BONUS 2: 10 squats immediately after the 100 downhill walking lunges.

Notes

- 2-Count High Skips = skip on left leg + skip on right leg. Skip HIGH ... max hang time. Always skip uphill.
- Backwards lunge walk: take a LONG step backwards. When you lower into the lunge, your back knee should lightly tap the ground and front knee should be over your ankle.

Hill WOD 8

Type: Long, Colors, Mantra

Instructions
All on a steep hill or whatever terrain you have to work with. Warm up first (always!).
- 2 minutes HARD
- Run easy back to start
- 4 minutes HARD
- Run easy back to start
- 8 minutes HARD
- Run easy as much as you wish

HARD = all-out time trial effort for the listed duration.

Notes
- Note the point you make it to on the 2min and 4min interval and make an all-out effort to reach it again on the next interval up the ladder by the same time. Then keep pushing hard to finish the full interval with the best you've got today.
- Great mind training opportunity in this one! It's a trip UP the ladder and requires perseverance to push hard on that last 8-minute time trial effort!
- Use a mantra or color focus on this one. When I tested this WOD, I used green as a new energy symbol, a red park bench I passed as a virtual solar energy push, and my blue shirt as a symbol to focus.

Hill WOD 9

Type: Downhill, Short, Tabata, Speed Walking

A downhill workout, really??? YES! Today's it's all about the DOWN ... well, at least until the bonus uphill part. This one is about overspeed training, while also offering a chance to focus on efficient downhill form.

Instructions
- Pick a hill that isn't too steep — gradual is OK. Warm up first (always!).
- Tabata DOWNHILL (8x20sec fast with 10sec rest breaks)
- 2min easy running
- Tabata UPHILL Speed Walking (8x20sec fast with 10sec rest breaks)

Notes
For the downhill Tabata, bend your knees more than usual and focus on a very quick cadence. Visualize that you are pedaling a bicycle in smooth circles.

Aim for smoothness, with a forefoot landing and a quick pull of your foot as soon as it contacts the ground. Stay relaxed in your shoulders, hands, and jaw.

Slow down after each interval by shifting your weight back and gradually scrubbing speed (vs. slamming your feet down as sudden, jolting brakes).

For the UPHILL speed walking, go as fast as you can without running. This is great training for hilly courses, especially ultra marathons, where it's often more efficient to walk quickly than to run.

Hill WOD 10

Type: Combo, Medium, Load, Weight Vest

Throw on a weight vest and go UP, then up and down (with squats), the UP again. Keep doing that until you finish your last 2min interval. Then add some short sprint starts. This one is a BURNER. You're going to love it and hate it.

Instructions
- 2 minutes UP!
- 50 squats
- 2 minutes UP!
- 40 squats
- 2 minutes UP!
- 30 squats
- 2 minutes UP!
- 20 squats
- 2 minutes UP!
- 10 squats
- 5 sprint starts (just come up to full speed, then wind it down)

Notes
- All uphill -- walk/jog down to restart each interval. You can do this on stairs as well.
- Wear a weight vest or weighted rucksack highly recommended for this one! Keep it on for the whole workout.
- When running downhill weighted, bend your knees more than usual and focus on a quick cadence.
- When running uphill, focus on maintaining an upright torso. The temptation under load is to bend over -- avoid this. Stay tall and keep the cadence high and legs springy.

Hill WOD 11

Type: Long

Just one interval in this session, but it's a LONG one! It is full time trial mode as you storm up a hill or a set of stairs for 11 MINUTES. That's enough time to enter the hurt locker and train your mental toughness skills in addition to stamina.

Instructions
- As much elevation (or steps) plus distance as possible in 11 minutes!
- Set a countdown timer and run UP, quickly, for 11 minutes. It's a full-on race to cover as much ground (distance and elevation) as possible before the clock hits zero.

Notes
- All UPHILL! You can do this on stairs as well. Ideally, it's a runnable incline. If it's too steep, then speed hike it.
- Use this workout as a chance to practice staying relaxed in the face of adversity. Relax your shoulders and neck. Don't fold at the waist. Make sure you're breathing full, especially on the exhalation, as the temptation will be to limit your exhale. This will ultimately reduce your oxygen intake while increasing tension in the body. Avoid that trap by breathing fully in and out.

Hill WOD 12

Type: Stairs

It's all about steps today, so this is a workout you can do even without hills! It's even possible with just a single step, repeated 1,200 times. I've you've got a longer set of stairs though, use it!

Instructions
Run up 1,200 stairs in as little time as possible.

Notes
- Single steps count as 1. Double steps (when you skip one) count as 2.
- Rest breaks are included in your overall time.
- Use this workout as a chance to focus on light, quick foot pulls. Relax your shoulders and neck as well.
- It may get especially tough at the half-way point. Decide up front that you're going to shift to turbo mode for the last 6. Approach them one at a time. When in doubt, take longer time on the recovery and really go for it on the hills.

Hill WOD 13

Type: Short

It's BLAST OFF time in this session with a series of 13 sprints, each about 13 seconds in duration. You're going to feel this one tomorrow!

Instructions
13 rounds of 13 second full speed hill sprint recovery on the walk or easy jog back to the start line

Notes
- Warm up with 10-15 min running
- Find a hill that's in the 2-4% incline range, not too steep. Our focus is on speed today.
- Mark a start line. Sprint your first 13 sec interval. Mark your finishing point. This will be your finishing point for the remaining 12 intervals, regardless of how long it takes you to get there. You'll get there in 13 seconds each time though, because that's your mission for today's hill workout!
- Use this workout as a chance to focus on light, quick foot pulls. Relax your shoulders and neck as well.
- START the sprints with a relaxed body, with the only tension in the quick pulls. You'll be amazed at how much wasted tension is typically placed in the body when sprinting. Use only the minimum necessary!

Hill WOD 14

Type: Combo, Fartlek, Sprint

Lunges? You want lunges? Whether that's a yes or no, you've got 'em in number 14! This workout mixes uphill walking lunges and Fartlek hill sprints. And just to ensure that it will suck the appropriate amount, it includes a 100-squat buy-in and 100 squat buy-out.

Instructions
- Buy-in: 100 squats
- 20min AMRAP uphill walking lunges, Fartlek style (do as many as you want) + double that distance in a hill sprint
- Buy-out: 100 squats

Notes
- Fartlek is a Swedish term for speedplay, which means the distance is spontaneously selected by the runner for each interval.
- The squat buy-in and buy-out are not included in the 20 minutes. Start the timer after the 100th squat.
- Your score is the total number of uphill walking lunges completed in 20 minutes.
- Vary the distance for each block of lunges you do — Fartlek style (spontaneously selected). Walk or jog back to your starting line and then do a hill sprint approximately double the distance you covered for the walking lunges. Walk or run back to the start line and set off on walking lunges for a different, spontaneously selected distance. Jog back and then sprint double that distance. Keep going until the timer goes off!

Hill WOD 15

Type: Game, Stairs, Short

Number 15 brings in an element of play. It's a 15min AMRAP of as many short hills, stairs you can complete. This one is well suited for an outdoors location that contains a mix of stairs and hills.

Instructions
15min AMRAP, alternating between 2 or 3 hills or stairs, all in the 20-40 sec range to summit

Notes
- Spontaneously select your pattern on the go. For example, you may want to do hill/stairs 1 three times, then do hill/stairs 2 once and then do all 3 in a row. It's all up to you!
- Run all of them hard up, easy down. Push yourself, but keep the spirit playful and childlike.

Hill WOD 16

Type: Adventure, Stairs

The theme for this session is ADVENTURE! This is an excellent travel workout, so pack it in your bags the next time you are exploring a new city. I designed this workout for a visit to the ultimate hilly town of Monaco, on the French Riviera. It will work anywhere you can find stairs though!

Instructions
Run up as many stairs as possible in 60 minutes
- Count each step UP -- no repeated steps allowed in the count.
- Time includes running to find new steps!

Hill WOD 17

Type: Skipping

Experience the suck/joy of uphill skipping with this one ... and don't worry, there are bonus activities included to make this one even more challenging than it sounds!

Instructions
Complete six 200-meter uphill skipping sprints, following the pattern below:
- Interval 1: normal, fast skip
- Interval 2: 100m normal, 100m high, floating skip
- Interval 3: normal, fast skip
- Interval 4: high, floating skip
- Interval 5: 100m high, 100m normal
- Interval 6: normal, fast skip

After each odd interval, do the interval number x 2 of 2-count uphill jumping lunges. For example, after Interval 1, do two 2-count uphill jumping lunges -- six 2-count uphill jumping lunges after Interval 3 and 10 after Interval 5.

After each even interval, do the interval number x 2 of uphill broad jump. That's 4 after Interval 2, 8 after interval 4, and 12 after Interval 6.

If you stop at any time or if your form degrades during the 200m intervals, the penalty is 10 squats (for each break).

Hill WOD 18

Type: Sled, Load

This session brings us a healthy serving of UPHILL Sled pushes and hill sprints! It's a proper suckfest, thus it's absolutely worth doing.

Instructions
- Push a heavy sled 100 meters uphill.
- Every time you stop pushing, sprint to the top of the hill. Return to the sled and keep pushing.
- Repeat this pattern until you reach the top of the hill with the sled.

Notes
- **Sled Weight:** The surface area of your sled base, the surface you're on, and the incline will dictate the weight you use. My suggestion is to load the sled with weights/plates equaling your bodyweight (not counting the sled weight). To get the intended weight right for your situation, aim for a weight that is about your 10 meter (30 feet) max for an uphill push.
- **Recovery:** After you reach the top, walk or easy run back to the sled.
- **Time Limit:** If you finish in less than 20 minutes, then continue with a downhill push, pushing as far as you can, sprinting to the star line, returning to the sled and continuing the push. If you make it back to the start with the sled in 20 minutes, then continue the pattern back up the hill.
- **Bonus Downhill Sled Sprints:** If you want a burner finish, then drop half the weight from the sled and sprint back in five 20-meter sprints.
- **Body Position:** Your choice of a bent arm or straight arm push.

Hill WOD 19

Type: Adventure, Combo, short

This session offers a nature theme and a dose of functional training. The steeper the hill the better!

Instructions
- 1 hill sprint, then 10min run
- 12 minute AMRAP of 9 stone thrusters and a short hill sprint

Notes
- Must be done in nature, if possible on a trail and surrounded by trees or other plant life, rocks, etc.
- Aim for a 20 second hill sprint during the AMRAP (As Many Rounds as Possible), but work with the environment and use natural landmarks to help you set the start and finish.
- For the thrusters, use a stone, log, fallen tree limb, etc. Be creative and have fun with it. A thruster is a squat with the object held in front at shoulder height. At the top of the squat, drive the object overhead (using your legs and hips to create momentum) until the arms are locked out.

Hill WOD 20

Type: Long, Combo, Adventure

This session is all about storming a castle! This is a time trial effort, racing yourself from start to finish at max intensity.

Instructions
- Pick a steep UPHILL finish line that is approximately 2000 meters away from the start line. The more elevation gain, the better!
- Run as fast as you can from start to finish, with the energy of a good old-fashioned medieval castle storm -- minus the sword and hammer fighting, of course!
- When you arrive at the top, complete one of the following bodyweight challenges: 100 squats, 100 lunge steps, 50 burpees, 50 2-count mountain climbers OR scale down the bodyweight challenge and immediately complete a second round.

Notes
- Do a long warm-up, uphill if possible. Fast hiking is ok, but make sure it's at least 20 minutes long. Then go for the time trial!
- Cool down with at least 5 minutes of running and up to 20 minutes if you've got the time.

Hill WOD 21

Type: Downhill, Combo

This session is an exercise in OVER SPEED. It's downhill sprint time for this one!

Instructions
- Pick a hill that's not too steep: 2-4% incline is ideal. You need at least 200 meters, but a nice mile-long (1600m) hill would be excellent.
- Complete 8 rounds of 22 squats and a 200m downhill sprint.

Notes
- Do a long warm-up, uphill if possible. Fast hiking is ok, but make sure it's at least 15 minutes long.
- Focus on a fast and smooth stride, like you're pedaling a bike.
- If you pick up too much speed, stand up straight and even lean back some. Always keep it smooth, even if that means slowing down a little.
- Maintain excellent form on the squats.
- Cool down with at least 5 minutes of running and up to 20 minutes if you've got the time.

Hill WOD 22

Type: Long, Stairs

This session has two parts with equal doses of long burn and intense burn!

Instructions
- Complete a 10 minute hill climb at 80% of your top, high intensity pace. If you don't have a hill that long, then do hill repeats on a shorter hill for 10 minutes.
- Rest 2-4 min and then complete a 10 minute AMRAP of a set of stairs that is 50-100 stairs long.

Hill WOD 23

Type: Sled, Backwards

This session is a drag! Grab your training sled or something similar (such as an old tire attached to your waist by a rope) and then hit this one hard!

Instructions
Complete the following as quickly as possible:
- 4 rounds of 20m sled drag sprint + 20m sprint (no sled)
- 1 round of 40m sled drag sprint + 40m sprint (no sled)
- 4 rounds of Backwards 20m sled drag sprint + Backwards 20m sprint (no sled)
- 1 round of Backwards 40m sled drag sprint + Backwards 40m sprint (no sled)

Rest time is runner's choice, but is included in overall time.

Hill WOD 24

Type: Fartlek

This session is a 30 minute Fartlek-style hill challenge.

Instructions
- Warm-up and set a countdown timer for 30 minutes. The location that you start the timer is your starting point.
- Your goal is to run 10 hills or hill sections in 30 minutes.
- Vary the duration of each interval.

Notes
- The hill can also be stairs, but you must run a new section of stairs or a hill for it to count. A section can be as long as you wish, but must be at least 30 seconds long. Run hard up and easy down.
- Spread out the intervals with rest breaks to ensure that each is high quality (with sufficient recovery time) and that you take the full 30 minutes to finish all of them.

Hill WOD 25

Type: Medium, Combo

This session plays on THREE (as the Magic Number)!

Instructions
- Complete 3 rounds of the following:
- Run 3 minutes hard uphill
- Rest 3 minutes; however, that rest must include 33 air squats
- After the last set of squats, restart the timer and finish 33 burpees within 3 minutes. If you fail to complete the 33 burpees within 3 minutes, run one additional 3 minute hill sprint.

Hill WOD 26

Type: Skipping, Backwards

Instructions
Complete 6-8 rounds of the following:

- 20 UPHILL skips
- sprint UPHILL 50 meters
- 10 UPHILL Backwards Skips
- sprint UPHILL 50 meters

All Skips are HIGH skips. Think maximum hang time.

Rest 2-3min in between rounds

Notes
- This Hill WOD includes uphill skipping, both forwards and the slightly awkward backwards uphill variant!
- Use your foot pull (straight up under the hip) to maximize the height of each skip.
- On the backwards skips, think vertical instead of worrying about gaining much ground backwards and up the hill.
- All sprints are max intensity. Focus on maintaining a quick foot pull on the sprints. Keep your torso upright and hips OPEN (no folding over or leaning into the hill).

Hill WOD 27

Type: Weight Vest, Load

Instructions
- Load yourself up with a weight vest and strap on one tire or two tires to drag.
- Find a hill, and get yourself there with the vest and/or tire in tow.
- Complete a total of 10 hill sprints: 6 short distance, 3 medium distance, and 1 long distance.
- Run each of them as hard as you can. Recover with an easy jog back to the bottom.

Notes
- No whining. This is a proper suckfest and deserves to be savored, preferably with a smile.
- Suggested distances: short = 100 meters, medium = 200 meters, long = 300-400 meters
- This Hill WOD is designed to test you, to pit you against hills, weight, and tires! Don't let them win. Own them and own this hill workout!

Hill WOD 28

Type: Downhill, Short, Tabata, Speed Walking

Instructions
Complete the following, all uphill:

- 20sec sprint
- 10sec rest
- 40sec sprint
- 10sec rest
- 60sec sprint
- 10sec rest
- 80sec sprint
- 2min rest
- 20sec sprint
- 20sec rest
- 40sec sprint
- 20sec rest
- 60sec sprint
- 20sec rest
- 80sec sprint

In summary, it's a 20-40-60-80 uphill sprint ladder with 10 sec rest breaks the first trip up the ladder and 20sec rest breaks the second trip up the ladder.

Notes
- Use this session to train your mind. The default response will be to become overly stressed and overly tense with each interval. Activate the opposite preventative action: relax into each fast interval (relax does not equate to slow), spin your legs at a quick cadence, and relax your mind.
- This Hill WOD is a play on the infamous Tabata protocol of 8x20sec sprints with 10sec rest breaks. This is an ugly variation and a great opportunity to EMBRACE THE SUCK!

Hill WOD 29

Type: Partner, Short, Game

Instructions
With two people (Person A and Person B), complete Sections 1 & 2, all uphill:

Section 1 - *Sprint to me*
- Person A sprints choice duration, then walks
- The moment Person A walks, Person B sprints to Person A
- The moment Person B arrives, Person A sprints, while Person B walks
- Continue this pattern until Persons A & B have both run 6 sprints
- Then, do 2min easy running or walking uphill

Section 2 - *Slingshot*
- Persons A & B separate themselves on a hill at least 30 meters/yards
- Person A sprints choice duration, then walks
- The moment Person A starts to walk, Person B runs easy to Person A, then slingshots past and sprints choice duration
- The moment Person B starts to walk, Person A runs easy to Person B, then slingshots past and sprints choice duration
- Continue this pattern until Persons A & B have both run 6 sprints

Notes
- Person A = A, Person B=B
- Sprint distances are always Fartlek, which means the distance is spontaneously decided by each runner for each interval. I suggest distances from 30 meters to 200 meters.
- This Hill WOD all about training with a friend. So, grab a friend and hit this one together!

Hill WOD 30

<u>**Type:**</u> Fartlek

This training session is for those times where the last thing you want to do is train on a hill, but you know you need it! This session is named "But I don't wanna run up a hill."

Instructions

Complete 10 Fartlek hill intervals. Shortest 20 seconds. Longest 50 seconds.

Notes

- Run the first of today's intervals well before you're in the mood for it. Just get it done, out of the gate, charging hard.
- Rest period is up to you. In true Fartlek style, pick a destination and sprint to get there. Complete 10 of these and you're done.

Bonus: Training Plan Sample

I've included for you in this print edition a special sample of the training plan section in the Expanded Online Coaching version. This includes the Training Plan introduction and three weeks of structured, integrated mind-body training sessions spanning Weeks 1, 2, & 7. Please see the Appendix for instructions on receiving full credit for your print purchase if you'd like to upgrade to the Online Coaching version.

Training Plan Composition

Successful training plans achieve a few key aims. The most obvious is that an effective plan brings you to your goal, whether that is a quantitative improvement (running faster on a given course, losing weight, etc.) or an earned race finish (first ultra marathon belt buckle, run up a mountain, obstacle course race finish). Ultimately, that's what you want, right? To achieve a specific goal.

What is less obvious, but still very important, is that the plan enables growth and leaves you with a stronger mind and body that you can use for future challenges and a happy life in general. That's what I get excited about as a coach.

Lastly, I believe that a successful plan also guides a runner away from injury and burnout. If you are injured, over-trained, or simply burned out and not enjoying your running journey, there's no chance you will be achieving the other aims, so this is territory we want to steer you away from. Healthy, motivated, stronger every day – that's the mission!

This 10-week training plan targets both your mind and body. It includes 5 sessions per week. It's up to you which day you place each session during the week. Most sessions include a run, mind training, and strength training. Some sessions include only one or two of these activities. The totality of the training experience is very important. Each component builds on the other. The Mind Training supports the intensity and perseverance required for the running and strength sessions. The Running sessions are of course sport-specific and the most important for creating the adaptations in your body to improve your hill running performance. The strength training is a critical force multiplier, offering you gains in power, speed, stamina, and durability.

If you are already following a strength and conditioning program, such as SEAL Grinder PT or CrossFit, then you may omit the strength training component of this 10-week program. I suggest you read the strength workouts though and ensure that whatever program you're following includes something similar and the sufficient volume. The strength program for the first 5 weeks is body weight only. No equipment is required. For the second 5 weeks, I provide options for body weight only, as well as for using basic strength training equipment.

I suggest that you read the Guidelines & Definitions to understand how the plan works. I cover Frequently Asked Questions in this section as well. Then, read through the first couple of weeks to get a feel for how the training flows. Next, commit to a start date, place some reminders in your calendar, and get started.

Commit to this plan, follow it with discipline, and you will earn that success. In 10 weeks, you'll be a different runner!

Guidelines & Definitions

1. **Session labels and duration of plan:** Sessions are labeled with the week number and day number. Session 1.1 is Week 1 – Day 1. Session 3.5 is Week 3 – Day 5. This fits the plan in its original 10-week design. You may, however, extend the plan to 12 or 16 weeks simply by taking additional rest days in between sessions and spreading the same number of workouts over an extended duration. If you chose to extend the timeframe, then think of the labels as phase numbers and do one phase after the other. Thus, 5.5 would be Phase 5 – Session 5, to be followed by Phase 6 – Session 1.

2. **Order of sessions:** I suggest you do them in the order I list; however, the day of the week is up to you.

3. **Missing a session:** As designed, it is a 10-week plan for runners who are serious about making quantitative gains during this time-specific time period. If this is you, then don't miss a running session if at all possible, and do your best to complete all strength and mind training sessions. If you absolutely must miss a session (due to illness, travel, or emergencies), then either double-up on a day where you can run twice with at least 3 hours between runs. If you are following this plan on a less aggressive schedule, then follow the sessions in order, without skipping any, just extending the timeline.

4. **Rest Days:** Take at least one day a week where you rest from structured training. It's ok to be active on this day, and I encourage it, but the mental rest is as important as the physical rest. You need it to recover, adapt, grow, and stay motivated.

5. **Standard Warm-up:** It is critical that you are properly warmed up for high intensity efforts. Before each session, run at least 5 minutes, preferably 10-15 minutes. During the last 2 minutes of

the warm-up run, add some progressively faster accelerations. This means increasing your pace and running 5-15 seconds at 60%, 70%, 80%, and 90% of your expected highest intensity in today's session.

6. **Standard Cool-Down:** Keep moving. Don't lay on the ground after high intensity efforts. Walk for 5-10 minutes, running at an easy pace if you wish. Then, stretch at minimum your hamstrings, quads, hip flexors, and calves for a few minutes.

7. **Order of workout steps:** In a training session, always start and end with the standard warm-up and cool down. The Mind Hack is typically integrated into the running component. Get into the habit of reviewing the future day's Mind Hack at least a day in advance, as some require a little preparation, such as reviewing the related Mind Hack section in Chapter 2. For the Strength and Core Training, unless it's written to specifically include it in your run or to time it before or after your run, then it's your choice when to do this during the day. Most strength sessions are best timed after your run, especially lower body sessions.

8. **Intensity:** unless otherwise specified, run interval sessions at your max intensity per duration. If you're not having to dig deep and tap into every mental tool you have, you're not working hard enough.

9. **Rest Breaks:** Unless otherwise noted in a session description, after each interval, rest for 1 minute. Stay on your feet during rest breaks. Walk and run slowly, and focus on deep long breaths with full exhales (until your lungs are empty).

10. **Benchmarks:** your plan includes two benchmarks. For both benchmarks, it is very important to select a course that you can repeat.

Your **Primary Benchmark** is a hill that is approximately 600 meters/yards long. It can be either a constant incline or mixed terrain. What is the most important is that it is a course you can repeat precisely. We will repeat this benchmark for a total of 3 times during this 10-week program. Record your time after each of the 3 benchmark sessions. Also record what mental tools you used (if any) and any other relevant feedback, such as weather, pacing strategy used, what went well, what didn't go well, etc. If you don't have access to a hill this long, then repeat a shorter hill (counting the time running up and down) until you have run up a total of 600 meters/yards. If you don't have access to any hills, run this on a treadmill set to a runnable hill incline. And if you don't have access to hills or a treadmill, run the distance wearing a light weight vest or weighted rucksack, or dragging a tire.

Your **Secondary Benchmark** is a hilly course that takes you between 20-30 minutes to run when you test it the first time. My intention is that it's roughly 2-3 miles (3-5KM) and is a mixed terrain, rolling course. You will also repeat this benchmark for a total of 3 times during the 10-week program. For this benchmark, warm-up, and then run the course as fast as you can. Again, record your time and other helpful details after each of the 3 sessions.

FAQ

1. **What is Tabata?** Tabata is an interval training protocol that involves performing 8 rounds of 20-second intervals. Rest 10 seconds following each interval. Tabata is used for running intervals, as well as for strength and conditioning training.
2. **What is AMRAP?** This is short for As Many Rounds as Possible. A 5min AMRAP of 5 air squats and 10 burpees means that you repeat this duo as many times as you can before 5 minutes expires.
3. **What does WOD mean?** Workout of the Day
4. **What is Fartlek?** Fartlek is a Swedish term for speedplay, which means the duration and/or distance is spontaneously selected by the athlete for each interval.
5. **What if I don't have strength equipment?** This plan includes 10 weeks of strength training without equipment. The 2nd 5 weeks also includes options if you have some basic equipment. If you have the requisite equipment, then choose the With Equipment option. Else, choose the Body Weight Only option.
6. **What if I don't have hills to train on?** If you live in a flat place or will be traveling to and staying in a place without hills during some part of this program, then you'll need to be creative in "making" hills.

I trained in Amsterdam for a year for racing in the Swiss Alps, so I'm familiar with this challenge! Stairs and treadmills are good inside options in the flatlands. I ran a mind-numbing number of stairs in a 16-story office building in Amsterdam that year, and it was very effective training for the Alps!

You can use stairs for many of the sessions in this program. Even if you have access only to a short set of stairs, just repeat it over and over to equal the intended interval duration. Parking garages are another good option, as the ramps typically offer a runnable hill. The same holds true for bridges and overpasses. Lastly, you can drag a tire and/or run with a weight vest. This is not a true hill simulation, but it adds resistance and a training stress that will improve your strength and conditioning for later running on hills.

If you have absolutely no option for running on an incline, indoors or out, then do the sessions as written on flat land, BUT ensure that you are doing ALL of the strength training sessions, preferably training with weight equipment.

Session 1.1

Run
Complete Benchmark 1 and log your time and supporting details (location, exact course, weather, clothing/gear). Don't hold back. We need your best possible time today.

Mind Hack
None today. Mind Training starts on Session 3.

Strength / Core / Conditioning
None today

Session 1.2

Run
Complete Benchmark 2: Run a 20-30 minute hilly course and log your time and supporting details (location, exact course, weather, clothing/gear). Don't hold back. We need your best possible time today.

Mind Hack
None today. Mind Training starts on Session 3.

Strength / Core / Conditioning
30-40 Air Squats

Session 1.3

Run

- Hill WOD 1: *Down the Ladder*
- Run UPHILL as fast as you can for each of the following intervals: 100sec, 90sec, 80sec, 70sec, 60 … to 10sec.
- Increase your pace with each interval.
- Rest exactly 90sec in between each. Spice it up by including a 30sec squat hold during each 90sec break.

Mind Hack

Mantra—Mind Hack #3: Select one mantra from the list in Chapter 2 or use your own. Repeat this mantra in your mind during each interval.

Strength / Core / Conditioning

Skipping: Remind yourself how to skip today by skipping for a total of 3 minutes. This isn't rope-skipping, but alternate leg skipping where you hop in the air pulling one foot up with a bent knee, while the other leg is straight. It's kid-style skipping or what you may have seen track athletes warming up with. After finding your skip for 1 minute, spend 2 minutes alternating between skipping and Running. Try to mirror the feel of skipping (relaxed ankles and forefoot landing) when you transition from skipping to Running.

Session 1.4

Run

Rest Day or easy pace, non-hilly 20-30min Run.

Mind Hack

Visualization—Mind Hack #4: Spend 2min visualizing yourself Running Benchmark 1 stronger and faster than you felt during the test. Make sure you paint a picture in your mind that includes details, such as the look in your eyes, your body language, your breath, and your finishing time.

Strength / Core / Conditioning

Complete 30 lunge steps per leg.

Session 1.5

Run
Rest Day: No Running

Mind Hack
None today

Strength / Core / Conditioning
20 2-count Flutter Kicks, 2 minutes in a plank

Session 2.1

Run
Complete the following, all uphill:
- 20sec sprint
- 10sec rest
- 40sec sprint
- 10sec rest
- 60sec sprint
- 10sec rest
- 80sec sprint

- 2min rest

- 20sec sprint
- 20sec rest
- 40sec sprint
- 20sec rest
- 60sec sprint
- 20sec rest
- 80sec sprint

In summary, it's a 20-40-60-80 uphill sprint ladder with 10 sec rest breaks the first trip up the ladder and 20sec rest breaks the second trip up the ladder.

See *Hill WOD 28* for more info.

Mind Hack
Yes Hills—Mind Hack #2: Today's Mind Hack training is all about observation. Observe your reaction to each interval. Don't control, just tune in. Are you dreading any of the intervals? Are you excited about them? How are you viewing the steepness of the hill? Notice your facial, neck and shoulder tension—tight? Relaxed?

Strength / Core / Conditioning
50 Air Squats + 20 2-count Mountain Climbers

Session 2.2

Run
Instructions
- Buy-in: 25-50 Air Squats
- 20min AMRAP uphill walking lunges, Fartlek style (do as many as you want) + double that distance in a hill sprint.
- Buy-out: 25-50 Air Squats
- See *Hill WOD 14* for more info. As an example, for the first interval you may choose to do 20 uphill walking lunges. Observe the distance you cover. Double that distance and take off immediately in an uphill sprint for that distance. For the next interval, you try for 26 uphill lunge steps. After the 26th, you take off on a sprint for double that distance. Continue this duo for 20 minutes.

Mind Hack
Color—Mind Hack #8: Pick one color to experiment with today. Either wear that color, bring it with you and leave it in sight, or choose a training area that includes this color. Experiment with different ways to use the color, e.g. throughout the entire interval, just at the beginning, just at the end, early in the workout, late in the workout, etc.

Strength / Core / Conditioning
Hold a low plank (on elbows) for a total of 2 minutes. Break it into sets if needed.

Session 2.3

Run
Run up a total of 500 steps today. Focus on pulling your feet up quickly and landing on steps as quietly as possible. Break it into intervals, Running up as fast as you can without slowing down. When you lose speed, rest up to 2min and then go again.

Mind Hack
Color—Mind Hack #8: Pick a different color to experiment with today. Same as 2.2, either wear that color, bring it with you and leave it in sight, or choose a training area that includes this color. Experiment with different ways to use the color, e.g. throughout the entire interval, just at the beginning, just at the end, early in the workout, late in the workout, etc.

Strength / Core / Conditioning
30 Supermans, 30 2-count flutter kicks, 30 sit-ups

Session 2.4

Run

- 2 Rounds of an 8-min AMRAP (As many rounds as possible).
- Find the steepest, meanest hill you can for this one, one that takes 1-2min to reach the top or a designated turnaround spot. If you don't have steep hills, then wear a weight vest or weighted backpack and Run on any incline you can find. If you don't have ANY hills at all, then use stairs or simply a box to step up onto over and over.
- Run up as many times as possible in 8 minutes. Your time Running down the hill is included in the 8min interval. Partial distance up counts as well.
- Rest 1-2 min in between each 8min round.

Notes

- Aim to improve your performance each round. Push yourself!
- Practice setting micro-goals (Run to the next switchback, signpost or tree).
- Stay positive.
- Upright body, quick foot pulls
- See *Hill WOD 4* for more info.

Mind Hack

Other People—Mind Hack #6: Experiment with levels 1 & 2 today. Race someone and cheer someone. Take a friend along for this workout. If that's not an option, then visualize racing and cheering someone.

Strength / Core / Conditioning

60 Body Weight Squats

Session 2.5

Run

Cross-train today for 20+ minutes. Rowing, swimming, cycling at low to moderate intensity.

Mind Hack

Visualization—Mind Hack #4: Spend 2min visualizing yourself Running Benchmark 1 stronger and faster than you felt during the test. Make sure you paint a picture in your mind that includes details, such as the look in your eyes, your body language, your breath, and your finishing time.

Strength / Core / Conditioning

Complete a total of 50 step-ups today (onto a box, chair, bench or large stone).

Session 7.1

Run
Throw on a weight vest and go UP, then up and down (with squats), the UP again. Keep doing that until you finish your last 2min interval. Then add some short sprint starts. This one is a BURNER. You're going to love it and hate it.

Instructions
- 2 minutes UP!
- 50 squats
- 2 minutes UP!
- 40 squats
- 2 minutes UP!
- 30 squats
- 2 minutes UP!
- 20 squats
- 2 minutes UP!
- 10 squats
- 5 sprint starts (just come up to full speed, then wind it down)

Notes
- All uphill -- walk/jog down to restart each interval. You can do this on stairs as well.
- Wearing a weight vest or weighted rucksack is highly recommended for this one! Keep it on for the whole workout.
- When Running downhill weighted, bend your knees more than usual and focus on a quick cadence.
- More info in *Hill WOD 10*.

Mind Hack
Focal Points—Mind Hack #7: For intervals 2, 3, & 4 use the following focus points, respectively: Single Point Focus, Wide Scan, and High Speed Tunnel. The last interval is your choice of focal points.

Strength / Core / Conditioning
Bodyweight Only
- 3-4 rounds of 20 air squats + 20 lunge steps + 10 jumping lunges + 10 jumping squats

With Equipment
- Barbell Back Squats or Kettlebell Goblet Squats: 5 sets of 5 reps

Session 7.2

Run

6 rounds of 3 minutes uphill fast walking. Run down at an easy pace after each speed walking interval. Walk as fast as you can for each interval.

Mind Hack

Color—Mind Hack #8: Pick 3-4 colors to train with today.

Strength / Core / Conditioning

Bodyweight Only

- Complete a total of 100 step-ups (onto a box, chair, bench or large stone). Stand tall at the top. Alternate starting leg occasionally to ensure balance throughout the 100 steps. Step off the box with control.

With Equipment

- Complete 50 weighted box step-ups. Hold dumbbells or a kettlebell. Stand tall at the top. Alternate starting leg occasionally to ensure balance throughout the 100 steps. Step off the box with control.

Session 7.3

Run

Instructions

- Run up 1,200 stairs in as little time as possible.
- More info at *Hill WOD 12*.

Mind Hack

Choice: choose any Mind Hack you wish to train with today. If it's hard to choose, do a short visualization right before the session starts, seeing yourself strong and fast doing today's training.

Strength / Core / Conditioning

50-75 Hillseeker Burpees

Session 7.4

Run
Instructions
- Complete 3 rounds of the following:
- Run 3 minutes hard uphill
- Rest 3 minutes; however, that rest must include 33 air squats.
- Details at *Hill WOD 25*.

Mind Hack
Other People—Mind Hack #6: Train with all 3 levels today, in order. Take a friend along for this workout. If that's not an option, then visualize racing and cheering someone.

Strength / Core / Conditioning
Bodyweight Only
- 25 reps each leg of bodyweight single leg deadlifts
- 25 air squats
- 30 2-count mountain climbers

With Equipment
- Barbell Deadlifts 5 sets of 5 reps
- 20 Kettlebell Goblet Squats

Session 7.5

Run
Complete 5 rounds of
- 5 Sandbag Thrusters
- 100 meter/yard sprint
- walk back to starting line
- 5 Sandbag Burpee Jump-overs

For the thrusters, use either a sandbag or a weighted rucksack, which you'll squat with holding it at your chest, and then press it overhead at the top of the squat. If you have no option for equipment, then do 10 Jump Squats instead.

Burpee Sandbag jump-overs: burpee, jump over sandbag at the top of the burpee

Mind Hack
Yes Hills—Mind Hack #2: Get fired up for each interval with a positive affirmation about the hill. YES! GO! HOOYAH HILL! Use whatever phrase works for you. Say it out loud. Notice your facial tension in each interval – when it peaks, relax your face and smile.

Strength / Core / Conditioning
Bodyweight Only
- 12-10-8-6-4-2 each of Reverse CRunches, Sit-ups, Plank Toe Taps, Flutter Kicks
- After the 10-rep, 6-rep and 2-rep set, do a 15-20sec Hollow Hold.

With Equipment
- 12-10-8-6-4-2 of TRX Knee-ins, Kettlebell Swings, and Kettlebell Russian Twists
- After the 10-rep, 6-rep and 2-rep set, do a 15-20sec Hollow Hold.

End of Sample Chapter

Be a Hillseeker!

Thank you for your efforts and trust! I hope to see you out running one day. Until then, run hard, run smart, survive, thrive, and live the life you dream to live. And remember, in sport and life, Be a Hillseeker!

—Coach Jeff

Let me know how this book worked for you!

Please email me or leave a comment
on my Facebook Coach Page:
https://www.facebook.com/CoachJeffGrant/

Expanded Online Coaching Edition

Here's what you'll receive:

- The most current version of this book in the latest eBook formats, including PDF.
- Video instruction to teach the Mind Tricks, Techniques, and Strength and Conditioning Exercises referenced in the book. In addition, the video links are embedded directly into the book, so the coaching is right where you need it to be.
- Full 10-Week Hill Running training program that integrates mind and body training.
- Color photos, hyperlinks to additional supportive and motivational articles and videos, and more features that can only be offered in digital formats.

Flow State Runner
Special Offer

For readers of *Hill Running: Survive & Thrive*, I am happy to offer a 20% discount off the digital eBook version of *Flow State Runner* when you order directly from the online shop at Hillseeker.com.

Please use this code: hillseekerburpees

Appendix - Resources

Please visit this link for the latest list of resources references in this book and other supportive materials, including videos, articles, and gear reviews.

https://hillseeker.com/runhills

Want a Hillseeker® T-shirt?

Cool designs and worldwide shipping.
Check it out!

Buy a Hillseeker® T-Shirt at
shop.hillseeker.com

About the Author

Jeff Grant's passion is in coaching. He thrives on getting in people's heads and helping them build a powerful inner coach's voice. His first book, *Flow State Runner,* was released in July 2016. Jeff's second book, *Run Faster: Unlock Your Speed in 8 Weeks,* was released exclusively on SEAL Grinder PT in January 2018.

Jeff is an American based in Switzerland, in the Alps, where he is often found running up mountains and swimming across cold lakes.

Jeff has coached a wide range of athlete types, ages, and settings. This includes military personnel in 7 countries, special forces candidates, SWAT Teams, and sports teams.

Jeff has a 20-year background in endurance and adventure sports. He has finished some of the toughest events on the planet, including the Marathon des Sables (a weeklong stage race through the Moroccan Sahara), the Ultra Trail du Mont Blanc (a 166KM extremely mountainous run in the Alps), numerous ultra marathons, Ironman Hawaii and other long-distance triathlons, long-distance open water swims, SEALFIT Kokoro, and mountaineering expeditions.

Jeff is a qualified yoga teacher, with over 600 hours of teacher training courses and 22+ years of practice. He studied the Pose Method® directly from Dr. Nicolas Romanov and ran a CrossFit gym for many years. Jeff also earned a unique civilian instructor position in the Kokoro cadre, coaching at 15 of these grueling mental toughness events.

Jeff is an active supporter of charity work in impoverished Malawi and a participant and fundraiser for the Epic Charity Challenge Normandy D-Day event in June 2018.

Printed in Great Britain
by Amazon